DAN CAVALLI

BLUEPRINT
FOR MAKING
MILLION$

*Master Strategies for Success
in Business and Life*

Morgan James Publishing • NEW YORK

BLUEPRINT FOR MAKING MILLION$

ISBN: 978-1-60037-439-5 (Paperback)
ISBN: 978-1-60037-440-1 (Hardback)

Library of Congress Control Number: 2008902228

Published by:

MORGAN · JAMES
THE ENTREPRENEURIAL PUBLISHER ™
www.morganjamespublishing.com

Morgan James Publishing, LLC
1225 Franklin Ave Ste 32
Garden City, NY 11530-1693
Toll Free 800-485-4943
www.MorganJamesPublishing.com

Cover/Interior Design by:
Rachel Lopez
rachel@r2cdesign.com

Habitat for Humanity®
Peninsula
Building Partner

DISCLAIMER

Daniel Cavalli or any entities associated with Daniel assume no responsibility for the use or misuse of this product, or for any injury, damage, and/or financial loss sustained to persons or property as a result of using this information. We cannot guarantee your future results and/or success, as there are some unknown risks in business and on the Internet that we cannot foresee. The use of our information should be based on your own due diligence, and you agree that our company is not liable for any success or failure of your business directly or indirectly related to the purchase and use of our information.

DEDICATION

I dedicate this book to my fellow Australians and to all individuals around the globe who are willing to fight for their dreams no matter what they are confronted with.

This book is for those who continue to strive regardless of obstacles they encounter along the way, and it is for those who have the inner strength to continue, eyes always on their goals, until they achieve what they desire.

Most importantly, this book is dedicated to the people who are continually dismissed, underestimated, or ridiculed when they come up with a new, untried idea while trying to get ahead. It is dedicated to those people who strive to make something more of themselves.

These people, the ones willing to rise above the status quo, are the ones who have shaped our history and will forge our future.

THE AUTHOR

Dan Cavalli is an Australian businessman. His expertise is in the creation of businesses and building them to full potential. He is an entrepreneur and expert on small-business success. He teaches essential marketing tactics and sales techniques to increase sales.

Dan Cavalli, aka "The $140 Million Man," is listed as one of "Australia's Telecommunications Tycoons" and also one of the "Internet's untold Millionaires."

AUSTRALIAN FINANCIAL REVIEW"

Designer of the
"COMMANDO BUSINESS SYSTEM"
and
producer of the ABC's of Success: Business Basics!

*Australian newspaper the *Financial Review*'s report about Australia's untold Internet millionaires [abstract] http://www.commandobusiness. com/pdf/Financial_Review_of_Telco.pdf

TABLE of CONTENTS

CHAPTER 3: MASTER STRATEGY 2

Creating Your Earning Vehicle

Introducing "BURP"

Asset Protection

Developing Thinking Ability

Stages of Thinking

Negativity

Affirmations

The Golden Attitude

THE NUTS & BOLTS OF RECRUITING AND TRAINING:

How to Recruit Salespeople

Interviews

Designing Our Sales Training Course

Expansion: Going National

Promotional Path

My "Train the Trainers" Program

Techniques for Making Sales

Leads Turn into Sales

Develop Your Rolodex

The GO System—A Personal Lead-Generation Plan

The MOGUL

A-DNA

Lead Nurturing Plan (LNP)

FOREWORD

I t was refreshing to read a success story about someone who came from a poor background, grew up on a farm, and had no idea about business or finance and yet has become hugely successful in his own right.

Dan Cavalli came from nowhere and was suddenly in the Australian limelight in a big way. His is a true rags-to-riches story. He is not your usual young and energetic upstart who created a techno computer program to gain notoriety but a fifty-four-year-old with no formal education. He became successful the old-fashioned way.

Dan started his business journey late in life by identifying an opportunity in the deregulated telecommunications industry and taking action. Many insignificant markets around the world have created opportunities for thousands of people to make millions of dollars. The key is to identify these opportunities early.

Australian newspapers have listed Dan as one of Australia's Tele-communications Tycoons of the twenty-first century. The *Australian Financial Review* identified him as one of the Internet's untold millionaires. Dan is an expert in identifying opportunity, whether from an idea, a conversation with a stranger, or a comment from a radio announcer.

This is what opportunity is all about, and Dan says this can be learned. I believe him, especially when he is able to demonstrate how anyone with average ability can do well if they want.

There are many people full of hype who claim to be able to make millions, so much so that these words are treated with indifference. Dan outlines two nuts-and-bolts chapters in this book, detailing how he actually did it. He provides steps that readers can visualize and follow.

I think you will find this book refreshing and easy to read. It provides simple explanations of how to duplicate the ideas and techniques to boost your business or personal life to the next level.

Mike Litman
#1 Best-Selling Author of *Conversations with Millionaires*

HOW to USE THIS BOOK

Most people, myself included, have a difficult time remembering the key ideas and information shortly after reading a book.

The following is a practical method I myself rely on to ensure that I'll retain important knowledge I've read in a text. In fact, I've found it to be such a valuable tool that I've made it part of my training program for new employees.

Always keep a highlighter with your book and underline the following key areas:

- When you come across a **principle** that you would like to take on board, mark it with the **letter "P"** in the margin.

- When you read a **technique** that might help you, mark it with a **letter "T."**

- For an **idea,** mark it with an **"I."**

You now have a quick reference when you come back to review. Your next step is to simply write out all the **techniques, principles,** and **ideas** you've underlined throughout the book. Jot them down in the same order as the book's chapters, and label each section with the chapter heading.

When you've finished, you'll have made a précis of the entire book that you can easily refer to whenever you need. As an added bonus, the process of thinking about the information and writing it down serves to implant it deeper into your long-term memory.

But don't stop there. Take action. Apply the material you've learned—immediately. Act upon the **ideas, techniques,** and **principles** that you've outlined, and make them a part of your day-to-day life.

A WORLD

OF POSSIBILITIES

CHAPTER 1》 I started my career in the telecommunications industry in November 1994. I have always dreamed big. But I never could have imagined that in less than two years my business venture would turn over millions of dollars a year, employ hundreds of people, and become publicly listed on the Australian Stock Exchange three years later.

How could I have guessed that I would have such an impact on people's lives and the Australian telecommunications industry in general?

I am the son of a farmer, and I was born in Proserpine in North Queensland. My parents have worked hard all their lives; my father worked the cane fields of North Queensland from daylight until dark, year after year. They've lived happy lives, but they'd be the first to agree with me that they are certainly not blessed with financial acumen.

I remember many dark, chilly mornings around 3:00 am when I was awakened by my father's movements, the sound of the toaster popping, and the comforting, familiar scent of toast a few minutes later.

I'd pull the blanket up around my chin as the cold crept through the crack in the window near my bed, and I'd wonder to myself, "When I grow up, will I be doing the same thing as Dad?" Tears would sometimes well up in my eyes as I saw him walk back in through the same door long after I had eaten my evening meal.

He still took the time to greet me with a cuddle or hug and share some precious moments before he tucked me into bed. "You have to learn a trade, son," he'd often tell me. "You don't want to work hard like me. I have the Cavalli curse, but that doesn't mean you have to follow the same fate."

Time after time, I wondered about this "curse," why he couldn't get ahead, and why he always had to work so very hard.

The Wage-Earner's Trap

I now realize that my parents lived the life of so many other wage earners. When you work for wages, you get nowhere fast. You find yourself trying to survive, trying to get ahead, trying to win the game by working more and more and more. You rack up the overtime hours. You work an extra day each week. Maybe you even pick up a second job. Look around you. It doesn't work, does it?

Despite my father's warning, I had a slow start in finding a suitable business that created wealth for me. A friend kept trying to interest me in the telecommunications industry. He was doing quite well himself by capitalizing on the deregulation of the industry that had occurred around that time. He pushed, prodded, and even tried to coerce me into the business, but I simply wasn't interested.

At the time, I was devoting my focus and energies to my own sales business, and I had met with some success. My friend also gave me a call one day and asked if I would be willing to train a group of his new hires in selling telecommunications. He had travel plans but wanted to get his new employees up and running while he was away.

I was happy to help. I trained five of his people in the sales process while he was away, and I did so a second time with a new group of trainees a few weeks later.

Little did I know that this was his last attempt to recruit me into the business—and it was working. While training his people, it was easy to see the potential of the telecommunications industry. I decided it was time to take a closer look.

On November 6, 1994, I joined my friend in the telecommunications business, and I have never looked back. In the first eighteen months, I set myself a target, wrote it out, and recorded my progress daily. My goal for the company was $140 million worth of monthly sales volume at the end of the first eighteenth-month period. I started with zero, but by the end of eighteen months, we actually achieved our $140 million goal!

A New Beginning

Now here was the son of a farmer with no formal education and whose parents had no financial business experience. Yet I was capable of producing $140 million within the first eighteen months of being in the business.

What does that tell you? If I could make all this happen with my background, you can, too. Anyone can do it. By applying my rules, methods, and strategies and by learning from my personal experiences, you can make the same kinds of opportunities for yourself, too.

What will make you happy? Do you strive to be financially independent? Are you seeking to retire with security? Do you just want to lift yourself from the burden of past debts? Perhaps enriching your quality of life is what drives you. Maybe you want more free time and to be free from the burden of financial matters. Maybe you want more time and energy to meet new people, to run your own business, or to build and leave a legacy. Whatever you choose, this book is all about learning how to become your own boss, build a family business, and become the master of your own life.

I'm going to share with you the formula for success that has meant so much to me. These are the keys I've encountered over the years that have brought me such a blessed, happy life and helped build a profitable, successful business.

I am thankful to all those authors who have planted the seeds of ideas that I germinated into action. Along with my personal experiences and knowledge gained from years of trial and error, I now pass this wisdom on to you.

MASTER STRATEGY 1

ATTITUDES AND BEHAVIOURS OF THE WEALTHY

Millionaires' Attitude and Intellect

CHAPTER 2 》 Make no mistake about it. This is about personal development. It is about assessing the correct information about a topic and being able to sell your ideas to anyone you choose. This is the greatest gift or skill a person can have. Any amount of time, effort, and money you expend to develop these skills will pay off handsomely. Plus, these skills are necessary for the survival of your business.

Before we go into more detail, there are some other basics that we should cover first.

What to Learn from Millionaires

What truths and lessons can we glean from the success stories of those who are financially prosperous? Generally, people become millionaires in one of two ways. Many inherit their wealth. Such people may or may not have expertise in financial and investment affairs, because they can easily afford the best advice and guidance money can buy.

The second type is a valuable individual to study. These are the self-made millionaires who earned their way up from average or below-average incomes and lifestyles. By studying these extraordinary individuals, their techniques, and how they think, we can learn what it is that sets them apart. We can also learn how to implement what works into our own lives.

The first and most basic lesson we can learn from them is that earning millions has to be your goal. That's not what everyone wants out of life, and there's nothing wrong with that. But if it's not your goal, you're not likely to take the clearly defined steps required to make it happen.

TIP: To move to the next step, you must have the desire to do so.

I was working construction back in the mid-1970s, and boy was I sick of it! It was filthy, grimy work, and I dreamt of a collar-and-tie career in a nice office. My desire for a job change led me to a help-wanted ad in the newspaper that read something like this: "Divisional Sales Manager wanted—no experience required, full training is provided."

I answered the ad. It was for a personal development course called Dynamic Business Management, or "DBM." Rather than being interviewed for a position of employment, I ended up being a candidate for a training course that I had to pay for.

Doing the Time

The course instructor (and multimillionaire), Tony Green, said something I'll never forget. He said:

Based on the averages, a person won't be successful or wealthy until he or she is about forty years of age. This is exactly what happened.

I was around forty when I hit the million-dollar mark. True, I've known self-made millionaires as young as twenty-four, and I'm sure you're familiar with some young achievers too. However, experts seem to agree that a person needs about twenty to thirty years to accumulate that much wealth. This is presuming, of course, that he or she makes the right decisions along the way.

Where the Wealth Is

Marshall Sylver, an International author says that 80 percent of the world's wealth is controlled by only 5 percent of the population. Even more staggering is that 50 percent of the world's wealth is controlled by just 1 percent of the population. So the first step towards changing your mindset is to decide just how much of that wealth you want for your own.

TIP: I don't know anyone who has become a self-made millionaire from earning 9:00–5:00 wages alone.

Dress for the Role

Expressing yourself through fashion and personal style can be satisfying, and it can connect you to those with similar interests and tastes. But I don't know anyone who lives, say, a punk lifestyle with a red Mohawk and is a self-made millionaire working in the everyday business world.

Most people wear the costume, the wardrobe and style, of their role and status in life. The wealthy and influential are no exception. You stand a greater chance of becoming a self-made millionaire if you look the part.

Associating with as many millionaires as possible allows you to learn from those whose rise to wealth you hope to emulate. You'll gain the cheapest priceless lessons and advice you'll ever receive from anyone.

TIP: Act like a millionaire long before you actually are one.

Discover Your "Mother of Success"

Would you like a dependable silent partner who asks nothing financially in return? You've got one, whether you know it or not. Think of the "Mother of Success" as your signpost, roadmap, teacher, and mentor.

This partner offers no judgment. She does not discriminate based on your personality traits. She does not discriminate between the greedy or the generous, the educated or the ignorant, the wise or the simple, the kind or the good, or the self-centered or the bad.

Can Bad People Be Successful?

My wife gave up teaching to work for a company that operated petrol service stations. The owner—let's call him "Mr. X"—ran several such stations. When my wife interviewed for a position, he struck her as pleasant, nice, and a good boss. Because of this, she was thrilled when he picked her from the large pool of applicants.

You can imagine her surprise to discover that the rest of the staff did not share her initial positive impression of this "kind gentleman." Without exception, they disliked Mr. X, and most were extremely unhappy in their jobs. My wife, a very mild-tempered and well-educated woman, couldn't imagine what could be so horrible about the man who interviewed her.

But this fellow soon showed his true colours. The first thing she noticed was how he abused his staff. He docked a person's pay, for instance, if he or she was late to work by a few minutes. He took every opportunity to discredit them, and he treated them like dogs whenever he came into contact with them. And talk about stingy: during a company Christmas party, he gave his staff a gift that was merely a promotional item for his service station!

By all financial standards, Mr. X was very successful. He had everything that the rich could want: a beautiful home, a new Porsche, a new BMW, and showy jewellery. Yet he and his wife were both regarded as curs by all, with the possible exception of their family and their limited circle of friends. I ask you, why was this person so financially successful?

I've seen horrible people raking in the dollars, and I've met wonderful people who succeeded as well. I've also seen both good and bad people who are habitually broke.

These qualities of ethics and morality matter in how you want to express your life and what you want your life to represent. But they have no bearing whatsoever on the creation of wealth.

TIP: Financial success has nothing to do with how good or bad a person is. It also has nothing to do with whether they are a negative thinker or a positive thinker.

Why Smart Businesspeople Consider the Worst-Case Scenarios

Are successful people positive all the time? Some people like to ignore the negative realities that exist. But if one doesn't stay aware of the negative—the potential pitfalls and dangers—how can one avert financial disaster?

Commercial or public buildings hold fire drills, and passengers are shown safety videos when flying a commercial aeroplane. These are all necessary and important strategies for dealing with the possibility of negative events.

While you certainly hope a fire isn't going to occur, it is better to be well-prepared "just in case." This is a very sound strategy. Just because some people choose not to think of the potential for problems doesn't mean that accidents won't occur. Thinking positively won't stop tragedy from occurring.

Good, bad, negative, and positive—they impact many areas of your life. But these factors have nothing to do with your financial status or your ability to grow wealth. Feel confident in attaining success if you apply the other elements and attitudes this book will identify for you.

MASTER STRATEGY 2
UNDERSTANDING THE BASICS

Creating Your Earning Vehicle

CHAPTER 3 ≫ Creating wealth requires some kind of mechanism, or "vehicle," that is capable of producing income without tying you down to a job.

Naturally, there are all kinds of different vehicles to make money. Yours must be planted, nurtured, and allowed to mature before they will produce fruit. You are the only individual who can do this. Nobody else can do it for you. One of your first lessons in this book will be learning how to recognize these vehicles in order to develop your own.

TIP: You can't buy these vehicles. You have to develop them. That means you have to understand the concepts involved in growing them.

Temporary income

There are two types of income you can earn, and there's a wealth of difference between them. The first is called permanent income. The second is temporary income, and it is far more common. It's the way your friends, family, and even yourself earn a living in the workaday world.

Of course, we're talking about wages or salaried jobs. Temporary income is earned through salary, wages, fees, or small windfalls from places such as insurance claims or the odd sale of shares.

If your income ceases the day you cease work, you were earning temporary income. You've got to work eight hours a day and five days a week for your wages. If you break your leg and are unable to work, you don't eat until you replace your income.

It is as simple as that. It also means that if you are a salesperson and you stop selling, your income stops. Temporary income is something that is necessary at first, but at best, it will only allow you to get by.

TIP: Remember, temporary income halts the moment you cease working.

Permanent income

Permanent income, on the other hand, doesn't depend on exchanging your time for money. On the contrary, permanent income flows into your coffers whether you contribute or not. Royalty income, for instance, is a form of permanent income.

Every time a movie star's movie is shown throughout the world, he or she gets paid a royalty, or a percentage. Whether they go to work or not, whether they're sick or healthy, whether they're at home or travelling the world, their royalties keep depositing into their accounts.

Let's look at the Beatles. They haven't written a song together for thirty years, and yet their families and estates still receive royalties on the songs each time they are played to the public.

TIP: Permanent income is not dependent on whether you work.

Another example of permanent income is money that is put away in a trust that you don't touch. It produces an income which is paid to you on a monthly or yearly basis, and this isn't dependent on you working either.

Let's explore this permanent income concept a little further. If you were given the choice between $100,000 now or $1,000 a month for the rest of your life, which would you take?

TIP: People make financial decisions like this on a daily basis that affect their futures.

Do you take money in exchange for hours each week, or do you devise a plan for money to be paid to you on a regular basis for the rest of your life? The choice is yours whether to spend now, or invest in a permanent income stream that will work for you for the rest of your life.

TIP: Invest in permanent income methods and you will achieve financial independence and never have to worry about money again.

Permanent income also differs from temporary income in that the age of retirement is no longer dependent on putting in years upon years at your job. With a solid permanent income in place, you can retire once that income becomes sufficient for you.

This brings us to the question, is it only the aged who retire? I don't think so. With permanent income in place, you can retire at any time on an income that will provide a very good life.

TIP: Royalty income can come from interest-bearing investments, rental properties, and many other wealth vehicles.

Introducing "BURP"

I've talked about permanent income and how royalties are a form of permanent income. Royalty income is represented by the R in my **BURP** formula. The next point I want to explore is represented by the letter B, **Business ventures**. You should work as fast as you can towards obtaining a business.

I was enraged after reading a newspaper article that said one needs a lot of money to start a business. Although it depends on the type of business, many don't require a lot of capital to launch. And there are hundreds upon hundreds of businesses that one can start up with minimum capital.

One of the best and most cost-effective ways of doing this is through the Internet. Be wary of scams, though. The people who operate unscrupulous sites are ready and able to take advantage of the innocent and unprepared. You can ruin your life if you're not careful.

TIP: When you start a business, you must keep a laser focus on one thing— your business must make money over and above its costs.

Treat this lightly, don't show respect for this principle, and you will become a statistic. Statistics show that 80 percent of business fails within the first five years.

High Risk

Going into business is a very high risk. But if you take care of the basics, you won't be a business statistic. The next letter in the **BURP** formula is U.

Think U as in **You** must invest properly. And the only investment you should consider is one that has the power to increase value in a compounding and regular fashion.

Secret

It was Albert Einstein who said the greatest phenomenon of the world is the power of compounding interest. To understand this better, let's explore a financial decision that we could make. Would you rather have $100,000 today or one dollar a day doubling itself every day for twenty-one days?

Which would you choose? If you chose the $100,000, that's great; if you choose an investment that doubles for twenty-one days, you'll have over one million dollars. Now which sounds best to you?

TIP: Choose an investment that doubles for twenty-one days and you'll have over one million dollars.

Specific techniques on how to achieve this can easily be found by consulting advisers. We're only going to talk about the principles here.

Print Money

The last letter in the acronym **BURP** is P. P stands for **Print your own money**. There are thousands of ways to print your own money and turn yourself into an instant millionaire. This is not through illegal means, but you do have to investigate exactly where and how to find these vehicles.

TIP: A simple technique to demonstrate how this works is to look up the local newspapers in your state, city, or town and look at the areas for buyers and sellers of the same products.

If you wish, you can act as a broker between these people. You take your cut as you help people put their deals together. This requires no capital. It does require, however, a little daring and ingenuity. The newspaper is the most valuable resource for business opportunities and income potential that I know of.

Public Listing

Another way that is a little harder is to take a business to a public listing. You can be worth $100,000, but take your business to a public listing tomorrow, and you could be worth one million dollars due to how many shares (print your own money) you have in the business.

Asset Protection

You must protect your assets so that nobody can take anything away that you've worked so hard to earn. It's foolish if you don't. This means taking the steps necessary to ensure that nobody can successfully sue or damage you financially.

I like to call this having a "wealth safety valve." A wealth safety valve is a business or company legal structure such as a trust or limited entity that does several things. For one, it directs purchases towards those that provide you an advantage. It provides the structure for asset protection and also provides mechanisms for your tax planning, so you never pay more than you legally should.

I can't stress enough the importance of a wealth safety valve. I'm considered by many to be experienced in business, and yet one year I made the unwelcome discovery that I owed around $6 million in taxes.

TIP: The lesson here is that you need expertise in creating a wealth valve. Ignorance is not bliss. Ignorance can ruin you. See your accountant or tax-planning lawyer.

Asset protection is not discussed in detail here, but it is a regular item in my newsletter, The ABC's of Success. Subscribe to it at www. commandobusiness.com.

They're Lucky—An expression of the poor

Do you think that someone who owns a brand new Ferrari received that by luck? Do you think people who have a $3 million home are simply smiled upon by fortune? Do you think a person who is financially independent and has a solid, strong business gained all that because "Lady Luck" favours them?

People like to tell themselves so, but this is seldom the case. There will be that rare person here and there who wins the lottery, inherits wealth, or stumbles into precisely the right place at the right time. But here's a much more realistic rule of thumb that describes the way the world truly works: all things being equal, whatever you want, hope, or desire doesn't appear out of nowhere for free.

We create our own success

We already discussed the fact that most successful, self-made individuals didn't reach their success simply because they were lucky.

From what I have read, 70 percent of our normal day-to-day thinking is based on negativity and the contemplation of events from our past. Can you believe that? Seventy percent! I've also read that 70 percent of people may cause their own illnesses. Now I don't know if that's true or not, but that's pretty serious food for thought. If 30 percent or even 10 percent of people could make themselves sick, that's very disturbing.

That should indicate what sort of power and influence negative thinking has on our lives. Don't get mixed up here with the fact that being negative will not stop you from being successful. But now that we're armed with this knowledge, how do we go about using it to change our lives?

Developing Thinking Ability

When I talk about removing the power that negative thinking has over our lives, I'm not talking about that self-help, positive affirmations mumbo jumbo you find cluttering the shelves at your local bookstore. You know, they're the ones that believe the world is changed just because someone thinks positively, or they teach you to repeat to yourself how wonderful you are.

I've never found evidence that positive thinking creates miracles. Positive thinking does help you get onto the right level of thinking in the short-term, but it doesn't materialize your thoughts.

Some books and motivational speakers give compelling and exciting pep talks that fill the room with energy and hype. You leave feeling energized and pumped up. The longest these hyped-up emotions have ever lasted for me is about two days after the meeting!

It sickens me to see so many books and speakers exploiting those who are plagued with insecurities. After all, people who have spent their hard-earned money and precious time on such books are genuinely interested in improving their lot in life. It's a shame to see them wasting their money.

But if 70 percent of what we think is negative, what sort of chance have we got of overcoming these thoughts and winning?

TIP: We have to reduce the negativity as close to 0 percent as possible.

If we subconsciously say negative things to ourselves almost all the time, we will produce negative results in our actions. The only way to stop this is to constantly talk back to these negative thoughts.

And I mean constantly. Never let a negative thought slide, even on the days that you're sick or otherwise not at your best. Even when you don't quite believe your "talk back," do it. It's as basic as that. And it didn't take an entire book to tell you, did it?

TIP: If you put wrong data into a computer, then your calculations will be incorrect. Your mind works the same way. Here's the flip side—feed a computer the correct data, it will provide you with the correct calculations.

Stages of Thinking

Just as you're vigilant about what you say in your mind, you must be equally attentive to what you talk about with others. For instance, let's say you're in a shop. You look at the price of an item you're interested in, and you quietly say to yourself, "I've seen a better discount from ABC Company."

Let's say someone overheard you and piped in with, "Yeah, they're slack here with their discounts." This level of communication is what I call everyday language. This is "one-on-one" conversation.

TIP: The danger is not necessarily in what you say. Rather, the danger can be in taking in what someone else says and letting them affect how you look at the world.

You may have only been trying to be polite by verbally agreeing with that person's comment. But by doing that, you've likely accepted his or her mindset at that moment.

Don't participate in others' negativity

By engaging in negative comments, the individual is really asking for help. If you find yourself agreeing with someone else's negative remarks, you're harming yourself, and you're reinforcing his or her damaging behaviour. There's an easy way to avoid this, but it requires your best communication and selling skills—veer the conversation in any other direction so long as it's positive.

Take care of your own needs first

Everyone has a responsibility to take care of his or her own needs. Otherwise, others have to take care of your needs for you. This has to be our first priority in life. We can't possibly hope to help or take care of the needs of others if we're floundering ourselves.

Let me tell you a story. It begins inside an aircraft that's flying across the jungles of the Congo. The plane is packed with a cross section of people—husbands, wives, children—everyday people going away on holiday.

Tarzan

There was a horrible accident. An engine broke off, and the plane spiralled downward, crashing into the jungle. Tarzan was in the area and came over to see if he could help. Miraculously, all the passengers had survived, and none suffered anything worse than some nasty cuts and bruises.

The survivors, fearful they would perish, asked Tarzan to show them the fastest way out of the jungle. Tarzan said, "I'll take you out, but it's a five-week hike. There is precious little water or food but plenty of danger."

The survivors said, "We will do anything, Tarzan. We just want to get out of the jungle."

"OK, but if you follow me, you have to do everything I say if you want to survive," said Tarzan. They all readily agreed.

Hungry Children, an Agreement Tested

They trudged along that first day, and before too long, the children were saying, "I'm hungry, Mummy. I'm hungry, Daddy." Ignorant of their real situation, the parents turned to Tarzan like most caring parents would. "Our children are hungry," they said. "Can't you do anything for them?"

Tarzan cut down a few bananas for the group, but food was very scarce. The days went on, and food became harder and harder to find. When the hunger reached the critical point, Tarzan took the parents aside. "From now on, I want you to feed yourself first," he told them. "I don't want you to feed the children. The children will eat every other day."

These parents said, "We can't do that. They're our children. They're our life." Like most mums and dads, they were prepared to die for their kids. One man bluntly refused. "I've got to feed my child. I won't eat. I'll give all my food to my child."

Tarzan was equally blunt. "Then I have no choice. You're out of the survival party. You stay here. You're not coming with me, because you are poison to us all. And even worse, you're poison to the children."

Negativity

This person had already spread negativity to the others. The mums and dads gathered around Tarzan and pleaded, "Why, Tarzan? Why? We'd rather our kids have the food." Tarzan shook his head and shrugged his shoulders. These people only thought of themselves as mums and dads. They didn't think of themselves as parents.

"You're all going to die," he flatly told them. "Do you know why? The children can't possibly survive without you. If you die, you've given the children a death sentence. Nobody else is going to put your child's survival above their own children's."

TIP: Feed yourself, take care of your needs, get where you want to be, and go where you want to go. Only then are you in a position to help others.

I built my business from zero to $140 million. You can bet there were shaky times. I purposely didn't share all of my fears with my business partner, and in the early days of the company, he wasn't aware of my troubles. It was a very demanding time for me and my wife in the beginning.

The biggest struggle was paying wages to our salespeople. Many times, we ended up using a credit card to pay our people for the sales they generated. In addition, we relied heavily on an overdraft despite running very close to the limit.

Consequently, I received nasty letters from the bank saying I better pay my delinquent house payments or I'd suffer the consequences. Even though I knew that was true, I kept telling myself exactly the opposite. You try doing that!

TIP: Say to yourself, "I feel good, because I'm doing the best I can."

You may not know how you're going to survive, but you do know this: the only way is if you remain strong.

Remember others are programming you whether you want them to or not. Whether it's through sharing their own negative outlook, lashing out at others, or attempting to give you ignorant advice, if you don't know how to deal with this, it's going to infect you.

TIP: Simplistic positive self-talk doesn't work, because other people are still programming you. This will neutralize your self-talk efforts.

Seventy percent of everything you say to yourself is negative. If you want to remove yourself from the negative programming, you've got to replace it with the positive.

For example, if someone says they don't like speaking to people they don't know, and you respond, "I don't like it either," just to make them feel better, they've negatively programmed you. The only way to fight this is to rebut it, even if it's only in your own head.

TIP: Always say a rebuttal to yourself to neutralize any negative statement that someone else has said.

Have you heard of the saying, "Birds of a feather flock together?" If you hear anyone talk negatively around you, even in casual conversation, stay away from them. They are poison to your personal development and business activity.

Overcoming Negativity—
Winning tactics to deflect a negative world

In his book *Learned Optimism,* Martin E.P. Seligman, PhD, tells of a controversial study that set out to test the hypothesis that people could be motivated by failure. The study involved experiments using dogs as test subjects.

Each dog was put into one of three separate large enclosures. The first enclosure contained a trap door that would allow escape if the dog discovered it. The second one was completely sealed off. The third enclosure was open, but it had high sides.

During the experiment, the dogs were continuously shocked with cattle prods. The dogs in the first enclosure reacted by running around wildly, desperately searching for an escape. Eventually they would discover the trap door and escape to the relief awaiting them outside.

The power of hopelessness

The dogs in the second enclosure were completely sealed in. Escape was not an option. After the initial frantic running about, these dogs did a curious thing. Despite the constant shocks, they simply lay down and gave up.

The dogs in the third enclosure were lucky. They served as the control group. Since they were not subjected to shocks, they eventually lay down and took a nap. Trial after trial, the outcome was the same. Nearly all the dogs in the second enclosure gave up once they realized escape was impossible.

The study's findings

The researchers hypothesized that people, like dogs, can also learn to give up. No matter what pain people go through to improve or achieve, the act of failing causes many to conclude that any further effort is futile.

The study's conclusions were largely met with scepticism by fellow scientists.

Testing the hypothesis on humans

But not everyone was so quick to dismiss these theories. In 1978, another research team decided to take the next step and devised an experiment using humans as the subject. For obvious reasons, cattle prods were not going to cut it this time.

Instead, the researchers substituted irritating stimuli for the painful shocks. In the first two enclosures, quickly flashing bright disco lights and deafening, high-pitched, abrasive sounds served the purpose.

Each enclosure also included a control panel wired to the lights and sound. Test subjects were told that the lights and noise could be shut off by entering the correct code into these control panels.

This wasn't exactly true. Some of these control panels were capable of turning off the lights and noise, but some of them were not. Those unlucky enough to draw the "dummy" controls would try for hours to get them to work. Eventually, though, they decided it was futile. Like their canine counterparts, they simply crumbled to the floor and gave up.

"I can't win."

Of course, we can only guess what the dogs were thinking that led to them giving up. But researchers didn't have to rely on mere speculation to gauge what the people were thinking. They simply had to ask.

What were these people saying to themselves before they surrendered? Can you guess? They were saying things like: "I can't win;" "It doesn't matter what I try, it doesn't work;" "I'm going to give up;" "Why should we stay here fiddling around with these buttons for another two hours when we've tried everything to make it stop?"

In short, these test subjects had learned the process of failure. It began with their negative self-talk and progressed until the despair was overwhelming.

Brain Babble

"Brain babble" is described as the total amount of thoughts that continuously pass through your mind. Amazingly, I've read that your brain babble can consist of one thousand words a minute. That's far faster than you can talk out loud. Think about the implications. If your brain babble is filled with negativity, that's an awful lot of failure-oriented words constantly flying through your head.

Learn to Succeed

So how do you replace learning to fail with learning to succeed? The answer is self-talk. But what sort of self-talk? You need self-talk to win. That's the only way to do it, and it works.

TIP: Negative thinking has some value. It often brings you back to reality.

The difference between pessimistic and optimistic thinking gives us the clue to how to change our thought processes. Just because a person has made negative remarks, that doesn't mean they're necessarily pessimistic. Optimistic thinkers often have negative thoughts, but they are only expressed in the short-term context.

Say someone says to me, "I can't do well in business no matter what I do. I can't do it. I'll never be any good." This person is pessimistic. But someone who tells me, "Last week was terrible, but I have a plan for next week that is bound to make it better," has engaged in negative talk combined with optimistic thinking.

The difference is simply this: a pessimistic person thinks and speaks negatively in the long-term. He or she isn't describing a problem in the here and now in order for it to be dealt with. They're speculating about a future that they've concluded will be negative, yet they have nothing to base this assumption on.

I received the following e-mail from a friend that puts an interesting perspective on what type of attitude to have.

People Should Have the Attitude of Dogs

Dogs love it when your friends come over.

Dogs don't care if you use their shampoo.

Dogs think you sing great.

Dogs don't expect you to call when you are running late.

The later you are, the more excited dogs are to see you.

Dogs will forgive you for seeing others.

Dogs don't notice if you call them by another name.

Dogs are excited by rough play.

Dogs love red meat.

Dogs can appreciate excessive body hair.

Anyone can get a good-looking dog.

If a dog is gorgeous, other dogs don't hate it.

Dogs like it when you leave lots of things on the floor.

A dog's disposition stays the same.

Dogs never need to examine the relationship.

Dogs understand that instincts are better than asking for directions.

Dogs don't hate their bodies.

Dogs agree that you need to raise your voice to get your point across.

Dogs never expect gifts.

Dogs would rather you buy them a hamburger than have a lobster dinner.

You never have to wait for a dog. They're ready to go twenty-four hours a day.

TIP: To affect long-term results, you need to educate yourself.

How? The following section contains some clues. Edison said, "When you become quiet, it just dawns on you."

How did the icons, those giants of yesterday, accomplish so much in their lives? Some say you need a mentor, books, education, Internet, and other tools to become inspired. But Henry Ford didn't have an industrialist to inspire him. Andrew Carnegie didn't know any tycoons who could mentor him on how to become a billionaire. Edison didn't have scientists to show him how to become the world's most famous inventor.

From everything I've read, none of these famous people are known to have had a "success philosophy." But they must have had something—a secret or a special power—to achieve what they achieved. Presumably it was something the layman had not heard of or didn't have access to.

We do know a few things they did *not* do. This may unlock the path to discovering what they *did* do.

Alexander Bell and Elmer Gates, for instance, discovered that the brain is both a receiving and sending unit of thoughts.

Noise distraction

Imagine sitting in your lounge room and listening to twelve different radios tuned to twelve different radio stations. It would be impossible to distinguish between them.

You've heard it said, "That music is so loud, I can't hear myself think." A similar thing happens when you hear a stereo on full volume in passing cars or hear jets taking off at an airport. Noise kills any hope of listening to your thoughts. Conversely, there are studies that show some soft classical music can enhance thought creativity. That's *soft* music—not loud music that sounds like noise to the majority of people.

Noise kills creative thinking. Don't be naive about that. Have you heard or seen those rev-heads whose cars unleash loud noise disguised as music? Or have you seen the jogger with headphones on and the music so loud you can hear it five metres away?

And to top it off, some uncaring or thoughtless teenagers tell their parents that they can study better with loud music blaring in their ears. They're all fools. And the parents are bigger fools for believing them.

Silence

Edison was asked many times to divulge his secret approach to problem solving. He always responded casually, "When you become quiet, it just dawns on you."

Famed physicist Albert Einstein, in a letter to the Queen Mother of Belgium, described the source of his astounding computation and analysis skills: solitude. Leonardo da Vinci used to stare blankly for hours at a pile of ashes. J. P. Getty spent six months of each year in the quiet countryside. Howard Hughes spent fifteen years of his life in solitude. Dr. Elmer Gates had a specially constructed soundproof room built to use as a think tank. Charlie Chaplin sat on deserted beaches for hours at a time.

So why do these extraordinary people believe that solitude and silence are beneficial? Oscar Wilde gave us a clue when he said, "Thinking is the unhealthiest thing in the world, and people die from it like any other disease."

With so many thoughts going through your mind, so much brain babble, so much outside noise pollution, is it any wonder that we reportedly only use so little of our mind's capacity? There simply isn't any brainpower left!

TIP: Slow down your thinking process so you can tap into more of your brainpower and focus on the task.

If you can reduce all this inner and outer distraction by 50 percent per hour, then you've freed up all that brain capacity for focusing on achieving your goals.

TIP: You need to devote time and energy not to thinking but to slowing down your thoughts. You must practice techniques like affirmations and meditation that will assist you in this.

Affirmations

If I talk positively enough about the things that I want for myself and support this with a viable plan, then what I seek will materialize. The value of the plan is obvious. The positive affirmation serves as the drive. It focuses you on the motivation and provides the moral support. Neither can succeed without the other.

A good method of positive affirmation is to record yourself speaking the kinds of things you want your brain to think. These can include the things you want out of life or what you want to become.

You don't have to conscientiously listen to or study it. You don't have to hear every word. As long as it's playing softly in the background, it will automatically be recorded by your subconscious.

Some people need to continue their personal development, and they need to keep saying their affirmations every day for the rest of their lives. This is not because they are bad or disadvantaged people. It is because they don't have a natural character with qualities like ethics, loyalty, or truth, and they need to be reminded of social and ethical behaviours.

Some years ago, I came across an individual. I'll call him AJ. His house and car were on the verge of being repossessed. While he was supposed to have an income of $200 a week, he was working on commission and hadn't been paid for two months. He was in debt to his family and others. Have you ever tried to talk and act positively when you have such huge worries on your mind? It's a challenge!

Because I liked AJ, I paid off his debts and lent him a few thousand dollars to survive until he found another job. As it turned out, I shared my dream with AJ, and he became my very first recruit into my telecommunications business in 1995.

I didn't know it at the time, but AJ lacked self-esteem and loyalty and was unable to live without wealth and security. His life until this point was that of a total loser and a person overflowing with bad luck.

I have never seen anyone with so much ability and potential that was riddled with more self-pity and self-doubt. Eventually he improved his lot in life through affirmations. He completed my sales training but balked at applying the sales system I had designed. He didn't like using it and wanted to do it his way.

It wasn't long before he was making comments like, "I'm selling, but I am getting so many prospects saying no." It didn't matter what he did or what he tried, the result was the same. He began to say to himself, "What's the use? No matter what I do, it is not having an effect on anything."

He asked me for help, so we went behind closed doors and hashed it out. I advised him on the facts of life and success. I taught him what to apply to change his outcome and the accompanying affirmations. We came up with a plan and the positive words that expressed what he wanted to happen in his life.

He followed the plan and used the affirmations every morning and night. In a few short months, he was the number one salesperson in the nation! It got better and better for him, and his income jumped to almost $20,000 per month within a year. He always spoke of me with the highest esteem and thanked me every day for what I had done for him.

I'll tell you the rest of AJ's story later.

What you think causes growth or harm

Thinking causes consequences. What you've got to do is decide whether you want what you don't have or whether you accept what you do have.

TIP: Thinking causes consequences.

Have you read, *Think and Grow Rich* by Napoleon Hill? This book is a winner for readers who apply its techniques. I'm going to share with you some thoughts from this book about how to write an affirmation.

How to write an affirmation

Hill says you must define precisely what you want. It's not sufficient merely to say, "I want lots of money." You have to be specific about the amount of money. All you need to know are the steps to take:

- Write down exactly what you want.

- Establish a definite date when you intend to possess what you desire. (Some learned people say you shouldn't put a date on what you want, because if it isn't achieved by that date you may become distraught and give up. I don't happen to hold to that theory.)

- Create a definite plan for acquiring that amount of money. What are you going to do to get it?

- Write out a clear, concise statement about the amount of money you intend to acquire.

- Read your written statement aloud in solitude as many times as you can each day. Read it at least once just before retiring at night and once after rising in the morning. As you read it, see, feel, and believe you are already in possession of that money.

Hill goes into more detail than I can here. I heartily recommend his book.

The NEXT Philosophy

Most of these teachings that we've discussed are incorporated into what I call the **NEXT Philosophy.** It's a simple but meaningful acronym, and I proudly display it on my car number plate. It has caused many curious passersby to speculate about its meaning.

High achievers, leaders, millionaires, top salespeople, and the like are who they are because of their belief systems and the intrinsic value they assign them. The **Next Philosophy** is mine. Many people say success is achieved by setting goals and maintaining a positive mental attitude. But these make up only part of the picture. Selling and persuasion skills are even more essential.

There is a difference between the average person and a winner. The difference between an average person and a winner is that achieving goals means everything to a winner. This drives them on.

TIP: The winner may be disappointed and apprehensive after enduring setbacks, but they'll put that aside and move onto the NEXT event.

NEXT doesn't mean aimlessly going through life from one opportunity to another. It means you do your best with every task, every job role, and every customer. In fact, it means you do your best in every aspect of your life. But if things don't go your way at times, even if you've done your best, then your next thought is: **NEXT**. This is necessary to forge ahead.

<u>NEXT</u> Philosophy

Never accept no to your request if it will benefit all concerned.

Educate yourself about how not to judge others.

Xpect rejection and fear as part of a winning strategy.

Try again and keep trying if you have a great deal to gain.

DBM and Mr. Green

As a young man, I undertook a personal development course (mentioned previously) given by Mr. Green. The course was called "Dynamic Business Management" or DBM as it was commonly known.

This course was as mind-blowing to me as seeing the birth of a calf or foal for the first time. Even though I didn't agree with the way in which they taught, what DBM impacted on me would change my life. It was the catalyst for changes in my attitude towards life and money.

The course could best be described as an isolation leadership program. The candidates met and travelled by bus to an unknown destination, arriving late in the evening. We were stripped of any timepieces, phones, and writing materials and sent to bed without being introduced to anyone. Very early the next morning, I'm guessing about 2:00 AM, there was a loud, frightening bang on the door. Then a voice called out, "Get up! We are starting the course in five minutes."

The instructors led us outside and into the bush in single file for about four hundred metres or so. Some of us were still in pyjamas. We came upon a shanty with a light burning beyond the entrance door.

Through the window we saw traps and whips hanging on the wall. At the entrance we were stopped and told to sign a disclaimer that released the instructors from any liability for physical harm that may occur during the course. Like sheep, all twenty-four of the attendees signed the disclaimer. The wording had unnerved us, and we were all terrified, wondering what we had signed on for.

The next twelve hours were eye-opening to me, to say the least. My colleagues and I went in as strangers, but we emerged from the course as close friends. Some of these people are still loyal friends today. Our bond was created by this course held over thirty years ago. I won't go into what happened in this course just yet, but I can say that I saw some things I didn't know humans could survive.

The Golden Attitude

Mr. Green had a pet name for the attitude we adopted as a result of the course. He called it **"The Golden Attitude."** Your attitude or philosophy about life determines how well you will do here on earth.

Let's take a look at your own attitude. I'd like you to make a self-assessment to determine whether your attitude is one that will prime you for success. Don't worry if your score falls short. This will provide clues how to go about improving your attitude.

This self-assessment has been modified for my use. It didn't originate with me but was learned from a previous business I was involved in. Obviously you will have to replace the sample inputs I've provided with your own, but these examples can provide a guideline throughout the test.

The self-assessment below will assess whether you possess a "business person's attitude." To be impartial, you may prefer to have someone else complete the test on your behalf. Make sure you pick someone who is brutally truthful. If they're weak and afraid of offending you, your results will be misleading.

Good Luck.

Personal Attitude Tester (PAT)

Your Selling Skills	Your Personality	Your Communication Skills
Closing asking for a decision 15 percent		
Presentation of the product 20 percent	Personal or business Values 20 percent	Verbal skills 20 percent
Handling Objections 15 percent	Personal Philosophy 20 percent	Written skills 20 percent
Prospecting for leads 10 percent	Personal Beliefs 20 percent	Body Language skills 20 percent
Subtotal 60 percent	Subtotal 60 percent	Subtotal 60 percent
		Total = 180 percent
		÷ 3 average = 60 percent
	ATTITUDE	60 percent (Ave) X 90 percent = 54 percent

THE NUTS & BOLTS
OF RECRUITING
AND TRAINING

SPECIAL NUTS & BOLTS
SECTION A

>> **AS MENTIONED,** if you want to become a millionaire, hang around them, act like them, study what they do to make their fortunes, and glean from this knowledge practical techniques that you can apply to your individual circumstances.

I can't offer you the chance to hang around me. But what I can give you is the opportunity to learn from my experiences—both the good and the bad.

That in mind, I'm including two "Nuts & Bolts" chapters in this book. These special sections will consist of concrete, practical solutions for common issues faced when building a business. I'm presenting these to you through my own story of how my team and I developed my company.

These Nuts & Bolts methods will be more than promising theories on a page. You'll be able to see them in actual use and observe how they played out over time as my company grew. Understand that you'll be reading how I made use of these methods and strategies.

What we're aiming for here is for you to grasp the wisdom and themes at the core of what makes these techniques work. Then, you can adapt them to fit the requirements of your own business.

This first Nuts & Bolts section deals with the challenges of finding and training quality team members.

 ## *How to Recruit Salespeople*

Advertising in "Local Rags"

The rules of "help wanted" advertising for employees are very clear: if one way doesn't work, discard it and try something else. But *always* advertise. In the early days of my business career, I didn't have much money. I was forced to use the cheapest method possible to advertise.

I was fortunate to learn the ins and outs of cheap advertising in one of the first self-development books I ever read, *The Success System That Never Fails* by W. Clement Stone. You'll find a slightly modified example of Stone's advert method below.

> Exceptional opportunity to earn up to $600 a day for those who want to get what they deserve for the effort they put in, phone xxxxxxxx.

Note how Stone dangles a "carrot on a stick" early in the copy: earn up to $600 a day. The ad copy doesn't merely state the dry facts about the position offered. It tells the reader how this position can benefit his or her life in a direct way. That's what makes this kind of ad stand out from the crowd.

I made good use of Stone's technique and adapted it over time to meet the needs of my own business. At the time of advertising for recruits, most adverts I used pulled in between fifty to seventy responses at a time. Here are some examples:

Advert 1

PROFESSIONAL SALES

Earn up to $600 a day simply by helping businesses save money on their phone calls. The company is an established national company. We require two people to join our friendly sales team. Excellent conditions with full training provided. Phone xxxxxxxx.

Advert 2

SALESPEOPLE REQUIRED

Brisbane based Telco has top salespeople earning up to $600 a day giving discounts on phone calls to businesses. Easy work, enjoyable people, and full training provided. Phone xxxxxxxx.

Advert 3

PROFESSIONAL SALES

Exceptional opportunity for happy, outgoing person willing to work and earn up to $600 a day. We provide qualified leads/lists to call. You don't need experience in sales as we provide training. Phone xxxxxxxx.

Advert 4

EARN WHAT YOU'RE WORTH!

Local Telco needs top performers to join our existing sales team. Uncapped commission sees our top performers earning well over $7000/mth. simply helping to save SMEs on their phone bills. Immediate start. Phone xxxxxxxxxx.

Advert 5

EXCEPTIONAL OPPORTUNITY.

Are you a positive, self-motivated sales executive passionate about exceeding targets? Australian telco requires four champions! Uncapped commission– earn an excellent income helping businesses save money on their phone bills. Phone xxxxxxxxx.

For more details on how to build your business go to http://www. commandobusiness.com/training/dbm_intro_tape1.mp3.

If you have trouble accessing the link from here, copy and paste the link directly into your browser's URL field. It requires a password and user name so use:

UN: training

PW: DBM

Interviews

I asked each applicant who came into my office to list three references on the application form. As you would expect, this provided a method for verifying the candidate's experience and character. But you may not have considered what an excellent networking opportunity these references present.

TIP: I often invited promising references to come by and see the opportunity I offered whether or not the original applicant got the sales position he or she interviewed for.

Some of my very best performers were people I had met as references for other applicants.

Mass Interviews

When recruiting salespeople, conducting a mass interview saves time.

When people responded to one of my adverts, I would book them all for the same time block. When they arrived and were seated in the waiting room, I would approach the group and tell them I was running behind.

I would ask them if they minded me presenting the company's overview as a group. If they were keen to continue, I would often hold a second interview with them one-on-one.

Employee Referrals

Another time-saving method is to offer an incentive to existing salespeople (spers or dealers, as they were commonly called) to recruit others for me to train. J.P. Getty's principle of "leverage" was the primary technique I used to grow fast. I will expand on leverage more in the chapters ahead.

REFERRAL TRACKS (FOR SALESPEOPLE GROWTH)

The referral track was responsible for our astounding sales growth. I used it, taught others how to use it, and made it a condition that everyone in my team utilised it. Their sales applications were not accepted or processed unless there was a list of referrals accompanying them.

There are two types of referral tracks. There is one for sales and the other for recruiting new salespeople. We used the latter for every person that interviewed.

Full training on this method is available by logging into www.telcoblue. com.au. You can then access the information about the free eCourse. You will be prompted to sign in with a dealer number, and this can be easily obtained by following the instructions.

We used the recruiting referral track at the end of the interview process. I used it to get fantastic results. The best results I achieved from one customer were seventy good qualified referrals. Some of the referrals were telephoned by him for me, and the appointment was set then and there. Remember not all salespeople used the script as it is. It was too aggressive for them. You may consider a particular version of it. At any rate, give it a go.

Here's an example of a typical recruitment script:

> " (Name) , as I was able to help you with this opportunity, I was wondering if you would now help me. If I could help you think of some other good quality people like yourself that would benefit from looking into this opportunity, would you be kind enough to give me their names?"

IF THEIR ANSWER IS NO (AND IT'S USUALLY NO):

"That's fine, ___(name)___. Let me explain. I don't really expect you to know anyone who wants a career change. However, you may know people who are more likely to benefit from this opportunity than, say, professional people like doctors, etc. That's all I had in mind. I'll contact them to see if they're interested. Possibly some of them won't be, but they won't know until they see what's available to them . . . "

Talk them into it if it will benefit them:

It's OK to expect a no here. Human nature being what it is, most people will answer no. Be prepared for them and expect to have to convince them. Go all the way here.

Typical concerns you'll hear:

I don't know anyone.

I don't give out names.

None of my friends are in business.

TIP: People are conditioned to say no, so expect it!

Your Response:

So, do you know any _____? (And go through the prompter sheet you'll find later in this chapter.)

TIP: If they answer yes and provide you names, write them on your "Referral List" (see example below).

It doesn't matter how many you get now ask permission to use his or her name when you speak to the contacts:

"As I meet these people, would it be OK if I mentioned to them that you and I have met and know each other?"

If they agree, thank them for their help. However, you may get one of these common responses:

- I want to speak to them first.

- I want to see how it goes for a while.

- Leave it with me, and I'll post some names to you.

- I'm out of time now. Can we do this another time?

- Don't use my name when you speak to them.

Your Rebuttal:

"Fantastic! That's OK. I would actually prefer that. I won't contact anyone until you're completely happy with your situation."

"When I do eventually contact them, so that I won't appear a complete stranger, would you mind if I tell these people (point to the referrals) that you and I have met and spoken about business today?"

Prod His or Her Memory

Often a willing interviewee will need help coming up with referral names (or leads for prospective sales). That request is too broad and unexpected for many people to come up with names on the spot, and they'll simply draw a blank.

That's where the Referral Prompter sheet (below) can help. This tool identifies the sources of where leads can come from. Ask them questions from each line on the sheet until you've gone through the entire list. For example: "Who sold you your air conditioner?" Note their response on your **Referral List.**

Note that I have limited the prompt name categories on the Referral Prompter, so you can add your own categories that may apply better for your circumstances.

REFERRAL PROMPTER

CATEGORIES	PEOPLE YOU KNOW (Choose the ones you like)	WHO IS YOUR . . .
Address Book	Air Traffic Controller	Civil Engineer
Christmas Card List	Aircraft Mechanic	Claims Adjuster
Friends & Neighbours (Past & Present)	Anesthesiologist	Clerk
Relatives	Anthropologist	Coach (Any Sport)
Church Acquaintances	Antique Dealer	Collectors–Coins etc.
Organizations, Teams & Clubs	Appliance Repairer	Computer Operator
Contacts . . .	Who is your . . .	Computer Programmer
Work Associates (Past & Present)	Architect	Computer Systems Analyst
Year Book (School, University, Friends)	Armed Forces Friends	Conservationist
Interstate Contacts	Art Instructor	Construction Worker
International Contacts	Artist (Commercial/ Fine Art)	Consultant
	Astronomer	Contractor
Who sold you your…	Auctioneer	Cook
Air Conditioner	Audiologist	Copywriter
Alarm System	Auditor	Corrections Officer

Bicycle/Motorcycle	Author	Counsellor
Boat	Babysitters (Parents)	Court Reporter
Car	Baker	Crane Operator
Caravan/Motor Home	Bank Teller	Credit/Collection
Cellular Phone/Pager	Barber	Custodian/Janitor
Computer/Software	Bartender	Cuts Grass
Extracurricular Tuition	Beautician	Dairy Farmer
Fence	Best Man	Dancer/Instructor
Floor Covering	Biologist	Day Care
Glasses/Contacts	Biomedical Tech	Dealer–Art/Car
Hobby/Sports Equipment	Boilermaker	Dentist
Holiday	Bookbinder	Dental Lab Technician
Home Furnishings	Bookkeeper	Designer
House	Bookstore	Diesel Mechanic
Insurance	Brewery Rep	Dietician
Jewellery	Brick Layer	Dishwasher
Kitchen Appliances	Broadcasting	Disk Jockey
Land	Broker	Distributor
Luggage	Building Inspector	Doctor/Physician
Musical Instruments	Bulldozer Operator	Draftsman/CAD
Office Equipment/ Supplies	Bus Driver	Dressmaker
Pets	Business Owner	Drill Press Operator
Pool/Accessories	Butcher	Driving Instructor

Shed	Buyer	Editor
Suit, Ties, Shoes, etc.	Cable Repairer	Teacher
Superannuation	Car Assembler	Caterer
Tools	Car Pool	Chauffeur
TV/Stereo	Carpenter	Chemist

REFERRAL LIST

Name _____ Date _____

NAME	ADDRESS	PHONE NUMBER	CONTACT

For more details on how to interview and recruit for your business, go to http://www.commandobusiness.com/training/dbm_Interviews_and_ mass_recruiting_tape2.mp3. It requires the same password and user name as before.

Designing Our Sales Training Course

Our training method, of course, evolved with time. It wasn't difficult to simply attract people interested in sales. But they also had to be people who were in our target market for recruiting salespeople. In addition, they had to be interested in building a business, and they themselves had to be capable of recruiting quality salespeople.

Our three-day intensive business-building course involves three different types of training. In one of these methods, we take the dealer into the field for further coaching.

The trainee is under the supervision of a qualified salesperson and team leader. You will find that this overview doesn't exactly flow or encompass everything. But I can assure you that it would if you went through every module of the complete training session.

View this as a glimpse at the training involved in building my business. If you would like to learn more, go to http://www.commandobusiness.com/ training/dbm_field_training_tape3.mp3

It requires the same password and user name as before.

Promoting the Course

Our free course was highly regarded in the industry, so positions proved easy to fill. This was good in terms of the sheer numbers we were attracting. Unfortunately, we did not always end up with quality people for the company.

Our solution was to charge for the course with the understanding that the person would be credited their money back if they passed the program and joined our organization. This proved a smart decision, and soon I was conducting training courses of up to forty individuals every week in my hometown.

It was time to go further afield. This business was like a powerful diesel locomotive. We were gaining speed all the time. This sharp growth spurred me to plan our national program.

How the numbers stacked up

During the first year and a half of doing business, I trained approximately 2,000 students throughout Australia. Most of those who joined our company were part-time. However, we also had some full-time salespeople (spers).

The part-time recruits certainly helped build our revenues. Even so, the backbone of the company was the spers who stayed for the long haul. In the first year and a half, we secured about 130 of these full-timers, and it was their efforts and the efforts of their teams that produced the majority of our business.

ACTUAL CONDENSED EIGHTEEN-MONTH PLAN

No.	MONTH	TASK	DESCRIPTION	MONTHLY REVENUE RESULTS*
	Nov–Jan	PARTNER -Set suppliers and contracts -Recruit five new spers ME Self-education, preparation, and implementation of sales training course	PARTNER -Set up area for admin and organized equipment. -Created job descriptions, filled admin positions, and trained them in their role ME -Learned about the products -Wrote the sales course -Prepared advertising -Wrote sper's contract -Project management plan -Designed visual sales presentation -Placed advertising -Interviewed recruits -Trained them to write sales	Actively prepared for sales. No revenue at this time. [*this section is approximations only]

1	Feb	Advertising One training course	-Placed adverts twice a week permanently -Interviewed recruits -Booked them in for training -Appointed a sales supervisor	**A Spers** Five **Sales revenue** $75,000
2	Mar	One training course	- Appointed interviewers for recruits and booked interviews for training	**A Spers** Five **Sales revenue** $225,000
3	April	One training course	-Appointed interviewers for recruits -Booked them in for training -Introduced cadet training for trainers	**A Spers** Six **Sales revenue** $390,000
4	May	One training course	-Approved interviewers for recruits -Booked them in for training	**A Spers** Seven **Sales revenue** $585,000
5	Jun	One training course	-Appointed interviewers for recruits -Booked them in for training	**A Spers** Eight **Sales revenue** $810,000

6	Jul	One training course	-Appointed interviewers for recruits -Booked them in for training	**A Spers** Nine **Sales revenue** $1,065,000
7	Aug	One training course	-Appointed interviewers for recruits -Booked them in for training -Appointed five sales supervisors -Started training trainers in major cities across Australia	**A Spers** Ten **Sales revenue** $1,350,000
8	Sep	Three training courses	-Appointed interviewers for recruits -Booked them in for training -Two trainers across Australia in major cities -Appointed ten sales supervisors	**A Spers** Fifteen **Sales revenue** $1,725,000
9	Oct	Three training courses	-Two trainers across Australia in major cities started -Ten sales supervisors started	**A Spers** Twenty **Sales revenue** $2,250,000

10	Nov	Eight training courses	-Appointed national trainer supervising content and quality of courses -Four trainers across Australia -Sales supervisor to ensure quality of recruits	**A Spers** Thirty-five **Sales revenue** $3,075,000
11	Dec	Twenty training courses	-Six trainers across Australia in major cities -Appointed fifteen sales supervisors	**A Spers** Seventy **Sales revenue** $4,650,000
12	Jan	Ten training courses [actual number of trainings went down this month due to lack of resources]	-Five national trainers for monitoring quality and production across Australia	**A Spers** Ninety **Sales revenue** $7,050,000
13	Feb	Twenty training courses	Continued with the five national trainers for monitoring quality and production across Australia	**A Spers** 130 **Sales revenue** $10,275,000
14	Mar	Ten training courses [training was starting to be slowed down as I was meeting my targets]	Continued with the five national trainers for monitoring quality and production across Australia	**A Spers** 130 **Sales revenue** $14,100,000

15	April	Ten training courses	Continued with the five national trainers for monitoring quality and production across Australia	**A Spers** 130 **Sales revenue** $17,910,000
16	May	Five training courses	Continued with the five national trainers for monitoring quality and production across Australia	**A Spers** 130 **Sales revenue** $21,705,000
17	Jun	Five training courses	Continued with the five national trainers for monitoring quality and production across Australia	**A Spers** 130 **Sales revenue** $25,485,000
18	Jul	Two training courses	Continued with the five national trainers for monitoring quality and production across Australia	**A Spers** 130 **Sales revenue** $29,250,000 **TOTAL ACCUM REVENUE** $141,975,000

* ACTIVE SPER [A Sper]–A salesperson who passed the training and works part-time and produces sales. Average revenue: $78,000 per annum.

* FULL-TIME SPER–They are not calculated as part of the number of recruits trained. They are calculated on the number of new, active full-time spers

less those who have not made sales and who have become inactive and/or left the company.

* **Revenue—Revenue** is based on the rule of 78 (see definition below). The full-time sper produce $10,000 of sales each month for twelve months, according to the rule of 78 = $780,000 on average.

* **Sper Numbers Averages**—2,100 are recruited over eighteen months. 130 on average are full-time spers from those recruited. This is an average of 7.2 full-time sper's per month.

* **Total Number of Training Courses**—seventy

* **Active Spers**—1950

* **Full-time Spers**—130

* **Rule of 78** —Means that when a sale has been made, the revenue from that sale is made up of a reoccurring monthly charge.

To look at a chart of the Rule of 78 and see how it actually works, go to the rule of 78 at http://www.commandobusiness.com/Rule_of_78.php.

 Expansion: Going National

Dealer Promotion Path: Incentives for Advancement

Our recruitment success resulted in sharp growth, and that meant facing a whole new set of challenges. For instance, I had to figure out how to keep my people selling without increasing my overhead costs.

The answer lay in developing and promoting an internal management career path. The dealers/salespeople would still be in business for themselves, but each one of them could, if he or she qualified, strive for advancement in our management team.

A copy of my original promotion path is below. You may not be able to understand the acronyms or the brief explanation of the terminology. Try instead to grasp the theory and technique behind it, namely that my people were motivated by recognition and financial rewards.

Check it out, and see what advantages you can glean from it.

PROMOTIONAL PATH

Path	Requirements	Rewards
Regional Sales Manager	**ACHIEVEMENT REQUIRED** i. Completed company recruit course. ii. Attend Monday rehash. iii. Know company presentation. iv. Achieve $20,000 NLD personal sales. v. Achieve $50,000 NLD team sales. vi. Have 2 DSM's in personal team. vii. Manage 7-module training. viii. Maintain $20,000 month new business.	**INCOME POTENTIAL** Year 1 $250,000+ Year 2 $400,000+ Company will continue to build people in team. 5 percent initial income on DSM's team. 0.75 percent royalty on STD IDD Volume of DSM's team. 7.5% initials on personal team volume. 1.25% royalty on personal team volume.

| Divisional Sales Manager | **ACHIEVEMENT REQUIRED**
ix. Complete advanced training.
x. Attend Monday rehash.
xi. Know the Telcoblue presentation.
xii. Achieved $10,000 NLD personal sales.
xiii. Achieved $20,000 NLD team sales.
xiv. Manage 5 active people.
xv. Maintain $7,500 NLD month new business.
xvi. Manage 7-module in-field training. | **INCOME POTENTIAL**
Year 1 $110,000
Year 2 $200,000
Telcoblue will build 10 people in team.
7.5% initial income on team's volume.
1.25% royalty paid on STD IDD Volume of team |
| Dealer (Sper) | **ACHIEVEMENT REQUIRED**
xvii. Complete basic training.
xviii. Attend Monday rehash.
xix. Complete weekly success sheets.
xx. Attend five appointments per week. | **REIMBURSEMENTS**

• Qualifies for office appointments.
• Free use of office facilities. |

Glossary

STD and IDD: Telstra trademarks for long-distance calls.

NLD: Net long-distance calls on the customer's bill.

Volume: Total monthly $ billing of customers spend.

Dealer: Salesperson

DSM: Divisional Sales Manager

RSM: Regional Sales Manager

DSM's team: The salespeople the DSM is responsible for

Initial income: New sales up-front money paid end of each week

Personal team volume: customers $ billing volume for entire team

Royalty: Usually a monthly income every time a customer pays his or her bill

Rehash: Situation role-play training

Active people: Salespeople who put sales in every month

The presentation: A sales presentation

New business: A new customer

Recruit course: How to recruit (one of the many different training courses)

External Managers

My system was capable of adapting to make use of outside managers. They could introduce the system to grow their individual businesses from within while using our techniques and methods. This provided a career path for their own team.

 # *Developing a Training Program*

While I was still in Brisbane, I conducted all the training. I was teaching a class a week with an average of thirty recruits. It wasn't long before I realized this was becoming bigger than Ben Hur. Initially, I was keeping up with the training but just by the skin of my teeth. And I knew that any slowdown would have been a bad move for the business.

I NEEDED FOUR THINGS:

1. A replacement for me in Brisbane.

2. A second trainer for interstate training.

3. A strong incentive to keep a large enough flow of new recruits coming to support any additional trainers.

4. A successful solution for replicating this business nationally.

As I said, I wished to accomplish this without increasing our overhead. How was I going to do that? Previously, I could have turned to Mr. Green for advice. But sadly, he had passed away.

Mr. Green had taught me the power of the subconscious. I put the problem to my mentor and confidant, "The Master" as I called my subconscious. The Master was where I sought most of my advice. I present my subconscious with an issue before I go to bed, and The Master answers me before morning. More about how you can use this resource is found in later chapters under meditation.

Inspiration came from The Master by way of this thought: there is nothing new under the sun, so learn from what others have done before me. Look to history, and that will have the answer. So I returned to one of my favourite books by Niccolo Machiavelli entitled *The Prince*, and I found the solution.

Without giving you an in-depth history lesson, I will cover the main points. Historically, when conquerors take over states, principalities, or a country, they have three strategies for maintaining control:

1. Devastate the inhabitants.

2. Occupy the region and control it in person.

3. Set up an oligarchy—an individual or small group of people having control of the organization.

Machiavelli says the best way to expand without hassle is the third method. You can control a city through its own citizens, even if the inhabitants are used to freedom.

I chose method number three. This gave me control of what was being taught nationally. Also, ties with our head office were maintained for exams, acceptance, and recognition. Simply put, I still had control over what was being taught but didn't have to be there. The solution:

My "Train the Trainers" Program

I laid out my teaching methods in the form of policy and procedures. I then began training protégés, and they took control of the training nationally. I call this the "Train the Trainers Program." At that stage, I was halfway into the eighteen-month period in which I generated $140 million.

The Search for More Applicants

To maintain a high number of individuals participating in our training courses, I had to pursue another market. The unemployed or those looking for a new career presented a wealth of interested applicants. To entice them, I said, "We promise you a job if you pass the course."

This worked like magic. Most candidates realized that if they liked the course and believed in the cause, they could make a career of it.

If you would like to learn more about this online, you can access the eCourse that I designed for interstate salespeople. Full training on this method is available by logging into http://www.telcoblue.com.au. You can then access the information about the free eCourse. You will be prompted to sign in with a dealer number, and this can be easily obtained by following the instructions.

 ## *Techniques for Making Sales*

GENERATION LEAD AND DUPLICATION SYSTEM (GLAD SYSTEM)

GLAD is an acronym for generation lead and duplication. Every business must put into effect a self-generating lead system. The more ways to do this, the better. But it's important to start with at least ten ways of generating leads.

There is more to selling than personally speaking to customers face-to-face. You should market your service through as many mediums as possible.

TIP: Be smart and market through verbal, written, online, and off-line mediums.

Most businesses that I come into contact with use just one or two ways to promote their companies. One or two marketing approaches is not enough to generate a constant influx of leads and sales.

I believe it is better to use as many strategies, or "Octopus arms," as you can to generate sales. Start off with two arms, and make it your goal to achieve four arms. Once you achieve that, move on to six or eight arms.

The end result is that you'll increase your profits by at least 50 percent to 100 percent. I've listed below some simple ways to market. Pick at least one that you're not presently pursuing—or not doing very well at—and add it to your marketing strategy:

- Email sales

- Internet promotions

- Advertising

- Door-knocking

- Telephone calling

- Asking for referrals

- Up-selling existing customers/clients

- Centres of influences

- Direct mail

- Seminars

- Letterbox drops

- Post Office box drops

- Postcards

My salespeople operate under a system I call **GO**. This is explained in more detail under the heading Personal Lead Generation Plan further in this chapter. This system combines both the **"GLAD"** and **"Octopus"** concepts I mentioned earlier; thus the acronym **GO**.

The GO system encompasses the total successful lead generation strategies and concepts I used to build a business from zero to $140 million in eighteen months. Salespersons adapted the GO system for their own team, because the GO system could be duplicated.

To increase sales, one should consider automating a channel of leads that will feed you with prospects interested in purchasing your products.

Of course, this is going to leave you with a whole new problem. How will you handle the sheer volume of leads? That's where GO can help. GO runs on autopilot. You won't have to cold-call if you don't want. You set it up once, and it will feed you for life.

You will receive calls out of the blue from people who have heard of and want your product. Best of all, you will have leads waiting for you before you even arrive for work. What a difference that will be from what you do and have now!

My business changed the day I started using the GO systems. They enabled me to duplicate myself and multiply the results by a factor of seventy-eight.

In other words, I discovered how to turn sales revenue made once into seventy-eight times that revenue over twelve months. As long as customers keep paying their monthly bills, the revenue you make continues every year from then on, above and beyond the revenue generated from any new sales.

As far as I know, there is no other book or training course that teaches this. If you want to make a lot of sales rather than just making ends meet, you can fix this situation permanently and effectively.

If you want to see a brief overview of the Octopus concept, it is best explained at http://www.commandobusiness.com/octopus_system.php.

Leads Generated from Print Medium

Brochures and other print-based strategies can be powerful methods of creating a self-generating lead system. But they can also be an incredible waste of money if you don't do it right. Don't buy into a generic cookie-cutter concept, or it will blend in with all the other marketing noise. You must design print materials with the following in mind:

1. Create your message based on how your product will benefit your target customer.

2. Grab your target's attention and hold it.

3. Octopus your message to hundreds of prospects.

4. Consistently use each Octopus arms.

Each of the strategies you implement must attract your prospect's attention. You can't count on the hope that they'll simply pick up your literature, read it, and consider your proposal.

The information on each strategy below is limited, because there is a lot of required detail. However, there is enough here to give you a basic understanding, so you'll be able to apply these methods to your business.

Brochure Bonanza

This is a powerful technique for the "one-man band" or a small team. First, have brochures designed and printed. Be sure to remember the important factors I outlined above.

Next, either personally deliver them to your target market or have a letterbox drop company do it for you. It's as cheap as chips to contract this out. Then your job becomes waiting for the leads to come your way.

However, if you do the drop-off yourself, there is an added benefit. You have the opportunity to meet the recipient personally. You'll be able to connect a face and name in the future. Make a mental note of the name and business, and write the details down as soon as possible.

Brochure distribution is one of our Octopus arms. Our success ratios are along these lines:

On average, 3 percent of recipients call us if the brochure has been written properly. If we get around a 2 percent call-back, we know the brochure could have been better, but it is within the ballpark.

If you distribute about a hundred brochures, that's two hours of work. Then you can go back to your office and wait for the leads to contact you, or you can generate more leads by dropping off more brochures.

Not a bad idea, is it? The key is to keep distributing the brochures on a consistent basis, because it takes time before leads will contact you. A copy of the brochure I used (with the name removed) follows below.

PHONE CALLS AT VOIP RATES FOR BUSINESSES WITHOUT BOXES OR COMPUTERS

Ask yourself this question:

How long is it since I've looked at my telephone costs? The company is the only telecommunications provider who can supply the Virtual Voip Product plan.

1. No more confusion finding the right product

2. No more wasted money on buying connection boxes

3. No poor quality calls made over the Internet

The company provides value and service with aggressive pricing on all total solution products and services for small to medium businesses.

- **10¢ CAPPED NATIONAL CALLS***

- **10¢ Local Calls**

- **International calls from 4.5¢ per minute**

- **Up to 50 percent savings; written-quote guarantee**

- **No Contracts; hassle-free connection**

- **Talk on a normal landline to anyone, anywhere**

The competition in the telecommunications industry has created a buyer's market for businesses wanting better pricing and better service. Contact the company to connect to their #1 telephone product and save $$ for your business. For your free quote, telephone 1300-the-company (1300-835-262) today or fax your details below to 1300-733-393.

Name_____Business Name_____

Contact Number _____ Contact am/pm _____

Contact email address _____

This offer is valid until September 1, 2005 or until withdrawn. Conditions apply. To view terms and conditions go to http://www. telcoblue.com.au

*Between business hours, 7 am to 7 pm M–F; otherwise 10¢ per minute.

Fear of Loss Is a Powerful Motivator

People hate feeling like they missed out on an opportunity. You've probably felt this way yourself. Remember the last time you passed by a great bargain and regretted it for weeks after?

Copywriters and ad campaign designers understand this, and they put this fear of loss to good use for their clients. You can too. For this reason, try to make every offer "good for a limited time." Ask them to take action on it *now*.

Spotlight the Customer Benefits

Most promotional literature doesn't work, because too much emphasis is placed on information about the company or the technical aspects of a product. It's hard enough to hold someone's interest with a written sales pitch. But you're truly going to lose them if they have to wade through loads of information to answer the only question they're really interested in:

"How will this benefit me?"

Here's how it works. First, mention a feature. Then say, "How this will benefit you is . . ." Then tell them how the feature will change their lives in a positive way. This strategy works like magic. Remember, a prospect must be told to be sold. And more to the point, a prospect has to be led before they go ahead.

Enticing descriptions of the benefits and your offer (or offers) should be the only focus of your promotional material. If you feel prospects would find it valuable to learn more about your company, and this would make them more likely to take that next step and buy from you, simply provide a link to your website.

Credibility and Expertise Sells

When people deal with representatives, they have to feel they are dealing with an *expert*. So make sure you fit that role. And don't assume they will simply accept you as an expert. Your prospective buyers have to be told.

TIP: Remember, a prospect must be told to be sold.

Tell them and tell them again, until they think it was their own thought. Many people don't like displaying their achievements or certificates in their area of expertise. Don't make that mistake. If they enhance your credentials, they give you credibility as an expert.

Make It Personal

The last thing a prospect wants to see is "Dear householder" on an envelope or letter. If your strategy doesn't include the name of the recipient, rethink the strategy.

When you meet a prospect, always address them by name. This changes your status from a complete stranger to possible acquaintance. In sales, perception is everything. Forget that at your peril.

Prospects Don't Want to Be Pushed

A salesperson can push someone too hard into buying. It is easily done. The real skill in selling is ensuring the customer is pleased with his or her decision. They don't like feeling that they bought only because they were pressured.

For this reason, the smart salesperson will always tell the prospect that he or she isn't the pushy type. The decision is always at the discretion of the customer. You have to "tell before you sell."

Make It Easy to Buy

All the fantastic strategies in the world won't do you any good if your prospect has to jump through hoops to buy your product. You'll lose more sales this way than any other. Avoid this by using the **drive-through** approach, which is all about convenience:

1. Give them easy access to the product.

2. Give them an email address and telephone number.

Confirm your prospect's order by fax or email. This is a powerful method of doing business. The most effective way to maintain customer contact is by email. It's more efficient than faxing, and it allows for an easy, permanent record.

Focused, Motivated, and Consistent

With any strategy, you have to work hard, especially at the beginning. For instance, it's hard work to constantly market your product. You have to be dedicated every day without fail. This just may be your most difficult challenge. Never stop marketing, until it becomes a habit.

Use the Octopus system and develop as many marketing arms as possible. Keep them active no matter the costs. Write up a project sheet to monitor your results every day.

I had a six-foot drawing of a thermometer pinned to the wall of my office. It had all my Octopus arms listed on it. All twenty arms were filled in each day to make sure the tasks I had set for myself were completed.

This visual tool works great. It keeps you focused and motivated. In my case, this chart was the most important visible tool to my success.

The Telephone Tycoon

Smart use of the telephone is another important strategy for generating sales. How you go about it will vary depending on your individual situation.

When I was first exposed to the idea, I said it couldn't be done. However, I had the common sense to test it before I discarded the notion.

I decided to make the test more difficult than a fledgling salesperson was likely to face in a real-world scenario. I had to do these three things:

1. Call businesses that I knew little about other than the name.

2. Cold-call businesses rather than use referrals or warm leads. This means using a list that doesn't provide the name or details of the prospect.

3. Ensure the script I used was able to be duplicated, so in the future, others could do the selling without my participation.

After many script rewrites, I achieved these goals. It was so successful, in fact, I could simply tell the sales manager that I wanted 1,000 sales this week instead of 500. He knew he must make "X" number of more calls, and voilà, the mission was accomplished.

If you are in a position to hire a telephone tycoon, this will work for you, too. Whether you have a problem successfully making sales, or you just want to double your sales volume, the techniques above are your best course of action.

When my company first started, we did the telephoning in-house, and we were successful. When we desired to grow faster, we outsourced the calls, and the success rate percentage remained the same. We never have to worry about sales, meeting targets, or achieving gross margins.

We pay an external company for sales at a predetermined amount as they submit them to us. The choice of doing it in-house or contracting the work out will depend on your ability to pay up front for sales and the size of your goals and targets.

Leads Turn into Sales

How do you handle the contacts? What do you say to make the sale instead of burning the lead? If the sale is in person, how you or your people handle the prospect's initial contact with your company makes all the difference.

Below you'll find a sample telephone script designed for securing an appointment between the prospect and salesperson. For this example, assume someone has contacted your office and is speaking with your receptionist, assistant, or outside contractor. Remember, the goal is to book an appointment. Note how the prospect is directly led into that action:

"Thanks for your call, Mr. Jones. Mr. Cavalli isn't available just now. He has been very busy promoting the (product name). However, he is the best person to talk to about it. Mr. Jones, Mr. Cavalli will be available for about thirty minutes tomorrow morning but then not available until next week. I can make a booking now if that suits you."

Simple and effective!

Here is a review of your must-do's for success:

1. Create a brochure that gets results.

2. Make sure you provide an easy to fill out form and fax number or email address.

3. Set aside time to do brochure drop-offs, and do it consistently.

4. If possible, use a letterbox drop-off company to distribute your brochures. That will give you more time to take the calls from the brochures sent out.

5. When possible, hire others to make the telephone calls for you.

6. Decide if face-to-face appointments or over the phone sales presentations are best for you and your product.

7. Make the process duplicable.

Develop Your Rolodex
(BECOME A CONTACTING MACHINE)

When I first learned about this Octopus arm, I could hardly keep my excitement to myself. It's that powerful!

Say you had a list of 3,000 prospects that you knew by name, and they knew and trusted you. Who do you think these people would buy their next widget from if they knew you sold widgets?

TIP: If they know and trust you, they'll buy from you.

Here's the secret: for every prospect you meet, learn his or her name. Either obtain a business card or write out the contact information on a blank card. File these cards into what I affectionately call the Hot, Warm, and Nurturing Rolodex (RoloCard).

TIP: You can also file your contacts on your computer.

Once you have their details stored safely away, you must now commit to a date and time you will call this prospect and offer him or her a free gift. The gift is your "thank you" for the opportunity to touch base and see if his or her situation has changed since the last time you offered your product.

Their decision to buy will be based on whether or not they:
Bought your product: (Hot);

Weren't in the market yet: (Warm);

Didn't want what you had to offer: (Needs nurturing).

File their RoloCards based on these criteria. With their permission, schedule Hot RoloCards for callbacks every three months for as long as they remain a Hot prospect.

Contacts with Warm RoloCards should be called back every six months. When they buy, move them into the hot category.

Contacts which require nurturing should be scheduled for callbacks every six months, provided you have permission.

Don't let them forget you. There is a fine line here. You must remain familiar without becoming a pest. In the meantime, keep building this list. The more prospects you have, the more self-generating leads will come your way.

Another powerful way to fatten your Rolodex is to create a newsletter.

Pack it with truly usable content, and make it easy on the eye. Make it so worthwhile that prospects will eagerly anticipate each issue, and above all else, make it free!

Send your newsletter via email using a tool called an auto responder. An auto responder allows you to write your newsletter and set the time you want your prospects to receive it. All you need is a computer and an Internet connection.

A Tool to Pinpoint Lost Profits

Below, you'll find a survey that will help you discover weak areas of your business that are causing you to miss out on untapped profits. As you work through the "Forty-one Questions to Improve Business," note the items marked with an asterisk. Consider these critical "must haves."

FORTY-ONE QUESTIONS TO IMPROVE BUSINESS

1. Can you and/or your team name ten points of difference that set you apart from the competition?

2. Do you communicate the benefits of your product in five different mediums such as promotional literature, website, letters, etc?

3. * Do you have two telemarketing teams working—one for attracting new customers and the other for servicing your existing customers?

4.* Do you use direct mail to attract new customers?

5. Have you tested PR (public relations) to attract new customers?

6. Are your ads returning powerful direct responses that compel the consumer to contact you?

7. Do you advertise in publications that your competitors don't?

8. Do you use scripted words when contact is made with customers?

9.* Have you tested pay per click search engine advertising?

10. Do you use Internet advertising?

11.* Do you send regular email communications to your customers and prospective customers?

12. *Do you spend two hours training your salespeople each week, and do your key team members use leading edge sales skills?

13.* Do you have three effective lead generation systems in place?

14. Have you set up ongoing communication with qualified leads consisting of phone calls, letters, and emails?

15.* Do you obtain and use testimonials from your best customers?

16.* Do you have an excellent referral system in place?

17. Do you have more than thirty ways of obtaining referrals?

18.* Do you offer something of value to your website visitors in exchange for their contact details?

19. Do you know how to write an advertisement or article about your business that instantly grabs the reader's attention?

20. Do you have an email newsletter?

21. Do you have a birthday register for your clients' birthdays?

22. Are all members of your team trained in the best way to sell?

23. Do you rent or purchase mailing lists of your target customers?

24. Do you take amazing care of your current customers?

25. Do you include a "PS" in all your sales letters and emails?

26.* Do you communicate with your current customers to ensure they know what you have to offer?

27. Do you use at least twenty marketing methods to promote your business?

28.* Do you use ten different ways to market your business every day?

29.* Do you follow up mail outs with phone calls?

30. Do you know how your competitors market their products?

31. Do you put your prospects' interests first in every contact?

32. Do you focus on the customer's primary concern or challenge?

33. Do you give something of value to your prospects on a regular basis?

34. Do you demonstrate your expertise so they'll look to you for advice?

35. Have you provided proof you can solve your prospects' problems?

36. Have you featured testimonials with specifics about the results your products provide?

37. Do you have an explanatory brochure for your products and services detailing the benefits in terms of your prospects' interests?

38. Have you given your customers a valid reason to buy something else from you?

39. Do you have an ongoing incentive or promotion for customers to prompt a purchase?

40. Do you have a simple special report created to compliment your customer's business?

41. Do you continue to educate customers by using your products and services can help them?

TIP: Pick just six of the questions that you consider most important. Make them part of your system today.

Establish a full Octopus system for your business and add additional arms every day. Below, you'll find one of my most important tools. In fact, I mention the Lead Generation Plan throughout this book. It lays out the most common channels of marketing, so you can track your success in each category you undertake. These are action plans you'll enact with one goal in mind: increase the number of qualified leads coming through your door.

The GO System—A Personal Lead-Generation Plan

The Uncomplicated Sale

Most of this book deals with marketing and selling to small or medium businesses through a direct sales team. It does not cover the complex sale of, say, a purchase of $150,000 or more. That sale may require four or five consultative meetings to close a deal.

Typically the sale we enjoy is somewhere between $200 to $16,600 per month or, in other words, $2,400 to $2,000,000 per annum. This sale can easily be made on the first call. Certainly, it shouldn't take more than another two contacts whether by phone (inbound or outbound marketing) or face-to-face meetings in-house or on-site.

In the past and still to a large extent today, salespeople are asked to generate their own leads, make appointments, visit, and then close or sell them. This is generally done through cold calling methods. Cold calling has a very real, but not total, part to play in the marketing and selling game.

The old ways of generating business still work, but for some specialty products, there are better and more efficient ways to gain business than cold-calling. However, I know that some promoters and salespeople don't like cold-calling, so I will not expand on its virtues here.

For my views go to http://www.commandobusiness.com/pdf/the_myths_about_business_and_selling_finally_exposed.pdf._

The MOGUL

MOGUL is the acronym for the Master Of Generating Usable Leads. This person complements the marketing process. Good marketing is the number one component to business success and growth. All things being equal, marketing is the most important, but most neglected, part of business.

There are many ways to generate leads. Some are better than others. I can't claim to have used all the better ones. However, I will share with you the ones I have used to great advantage. To understand how a MOGUL uses leads, you have to realize that marketing is not selling. For the MOGUL, he knows that he must eventually pass a lead over to the sales team.

The marketing and selling roles (although sometimes these roles can be done by the same individual) are very different.

A salesperson, or sper as they are more commonly called in my organization, knows that if he or she is given either a qualified lead or someone who is viewed as a hot prospect, then he or she has the responsibility to make the sale. This is where money for his or her efforts can be seen instantly.

A MOGUL on the other hand knows that his role involves finding, qualifying, and passing on the lead. If the lead doesn't buy, the MOGUL receives the lead back for future nurturing. There is no money for anyone here. It is delayed gratification.

If a sper gets too involved in lead generation, he will starve. The sper would leave the industry and seek out a job with regular pay and so-called security.

The sper, for the most part, in my type of business is commonly a commissioned agent. The MOGUL is generally on a base salary with a commissioned bonus based on results. The reason his or her pay is structured that way is because it assimilates the roles that each play. The sper is a short-term hunter, and the MOGUL is a long-term relationship maker and trust builder.

The role and the pay structure dictates that the two types of character are different, and it is unwise to marry them in one individual role, except in certain circumstances.

MOGULS know an enquiry is not a lead

There is more to making a sale than just receiving an enquiry. An enquiry is an interested person that has asked for some information or has been asked for information face-to-face, and they have given it willingly. When I talk about an enquiry, I also include in that definition the very first verbal contact with a person from inbound or outbound marketing.

It is not hard to generate enquiries or make contacts. The art is sorting through the enquiries, turning them into leads, and then turning them into motivated leads while updating and managing your database. The last step is turning it over to the sales department or a sper as a qualified prospect ready to buy.

A MOGULS job consists of finding enquiries, creating leads, building relationships, and instilling trust. They must also nurture leads until they are ready for the sales process.

If the lead comes from an advert (which has given enough details to buy, and all the person has to do is provide credit card details), then the sales success ratio goes up to eight out of ten (including cancellations). On the other hand, if the lead requires further consultation and more information, the sales success ratio can move back to one in ten.

Depending on the enquiries' source, it will take about five enquiries on average to produce one qualified lead. Leads on the other hand are willing prospects that have indicated they want to know more about your product. This is where the MOGUL really begins his or her work in the lead management process.

As I mentioned before, a lead can be cold, warm, or hot. This classification indicates how qualified the lead is at any point in the lead generation process. Cold means the lead is just out of the enquiry stage and wants more information. Warm means they have accepted the information as relevant and are considering their options, but they are not yet considered ready for the sales process.

A-DNA

A-DNA is the acronym (not in order of priority) for:

1. Afford it

2. Decision-maker

3. Need

4. Appointment or sales ready

Hot leads are those that have had an A-DNA test. They are qualified by all four steps and are able to buy. Hot is the only stage in which a lead gets turned over to the sales team to begin the sales process.

This doesn't mean the hot lead will simply sign on the dotted line. It will still take a salesperson to skillfully entice the hot lead into the buying cycle and persuasively close the deal.

Let's take a look at exactly what A-DNA means in detail.

QUALIFICATION	DESCRIPTION	FOLLOW-UP
Afford it	Does the prospect have the ability to pay for the product? Are they gainfully employed? Can they manage a deposit? Other questions to find out if they are able to pay for your product.	If not, slide them back into the **Lead Nurturing Process** until they are ready.

Decision-maker	Does this prospect have the authority to make the purchase? Do they have to check with another party? Are they the business owner? Other questions to find out if they are able to make the decision to buy your product.	If not, slide them back into the **Lead Nurturing Process** until they can arrange for the authority to buy.
Need	Does this prospect have a need for your product? Have they given you the reasons why they could use it? Other questions to find out if they need your product.	If not, slide them back into the **Lead Nurturing Process** until they have developed the need to buy.
Appointment or sales ready	Has this prospect indicated he or she will go to the next step? Have you tested if he or she will see a salesperson? Are they sales ready? Other questions to find out if they are ready to buy.	If not, slide them back into the **Lead Nurturing Process** until they have indicated they are ready to buy.

Once the lead is qualified as hot and has been given to the sales department, it doesn't mean the sale will be made. If the sales department can't sell them, they are given back to the MOGUL to nurture that prospect again. The MOGUL readies the lead for another sales attempt sometime in the future or until the lead says goodbye.

To be successful in this day and age, the old ways of selling have to be reconsidered. The reason for the change is the Internet. Today your prospect has been inundated with information and marketing messages from your competition. They can also access information directly by surfing the net themselves.

However, all things being equal, there are people interested in what you have to sell. You just don't know who they are. In a metropolis of two million people, let's say you will have about 20,000 prospects looking for what you have to sell. Accordingly, there will also be another 20,000 that may be interested in looking at you product.

In order to have the advantage, you have to differentiate yourself from the others. You must preempt business by making the contact and nurturing leads until they are ready, willing, and able to buy from you and not the opposition. Your prime objective is to attract, find, and create leads that look to you as the expert.

You do this through the MOGULS and the lead nurturing process using your points of difference (the services or product differences that are usually better than your competitors') from your competition. It is advantageous to develop those points of difference into a well-defined statement of what you can offer your prospects. Then you are ready to start generating leads.

The Crab Pot

The crab pot is the illustrative diagram of the process of the lead generation process. It can be found at http://www.commandobusiness.com/Go_System_Crab_Pot_2.doc.

Enquiry/Contact

This is the area that has to be concentrated on the most. You need fuel in the car to continue the journey. This is the fuel that enables you to get, hold, and develop a fantastic GO System. There are many ways to do this, and I'm going to discuss them in order of priority.

The Phone

People in business depend on the phone for running their business properly. Don't fall into a false sense of security, thinking that people in business don't want the phone to ring. We are not talking about a housewife or wageworker who is home watching television, cleaning the house, or doing chores that have to be done. Because when a salesperson disturbs his or her comfort zone by ringing to ask if they want a free dishwashing-liquid sample, it generally is at an inopportune time.

This is about the businessperson who wants his or her phone to ring in case it's potential business. It may be a customer wanting the product, an enquiry about some special deal, or some other potential business on the end of the line.

Some people believe you cannot sell over the phone. They think the phone is only good for setting appointments or gathering information. And some people thought the world was flat not so long ago. Believe it. No matter what product you have, it can be sold over the phone, provided you don't have a complex sale. As I mentioned, these strategies apply only to the uncomplicated sale.

I am regretful I didn't open my eyes sooner to phone selling. I wasted years thinking my product couldn't be sold over the phone. It took six months of perseverance and trial and error, but we perfected the system. And it took our sales from four hundred a month to four hundred a week with less cost and more profit.

It is such a useful tool for generating hot leads and sales, we have all but closed down our direct sales force and concentrated on building up the call centre. The sales success closing ratios for a call centre MOGUL are equal to ten direct spers in the field.

It has become so effective for us that we set up a special division that successfully amalgamates the MOGUL and the sper into the same person. In other words, because of the flexibility of the phone, the whole sales process is now handled by the one MOGUL.

MOGUL Techniques

The MOGUL is a much specialised individual and has the skills necessary to create and nurture leads until they qualify as a hot lead through the **LNP** (lead-nurturing plan). MOGULs also have the skills to follow through and make a sale. The techniques they use are teachable, and I will outline some of the more dominant skills they possess:

1. They view the process of GO as a long-term investment. They don't just make one hundred calls and give up. A MOGUL will not invest time and money into the system and then abandon it after a few weeks like most other individuals.

2. They never throw away or give up on a lead until the prospect either buys or says not to call anymore.

3. They will not terminate the call just because the decision-maker is not available at that time.

Rather, they use that time with the recipient to gain valuable information about the decision-maker. They also use this time to determine if there is another person in the business capable of participating in the decision-making process. They will build a relationship with any person that can help them reach their goal.

1. They recognize that the higher they get in the hierarchy, the better chance they have of building a hot lead ready for a sale.

2. They realize that the important thing is to get the recipient to enter the LNP program. First, they ask permission to email them information. Then, once they are in the LNP, they are well on the way to building a relationship and gaining the sale.

I've spent thousands of dollars on advertising through radio, direct mail, magazines, local newspapers, and national newspapers. And without a doubt, the phone method of advertising, lead generation, lead nurturing, and sales generating is the best.

It is for this reason that I will build on the phone system and its associated extensions of lead generating. I do expand, however, on other direct channels when I explain the **GO System** in other parts of the book.

EMAIL

Email can be used closely with the phone. Together, they are the most powerful medium you have for lead generation. A properly created email system can be a powerful ally in the **GO System**. This is done primarily through an auto responder system that automatically sends a series of templated emails to the recipient in the LNP.

To do this, there has to be a mechanism to gain opt-ins' email addresses from interested prospects. The best way is to set up a subscriber's box on your website home page and every other landing sales page. The interested prospect will leave his or her email address to receive whatever it is you are offering. Maybe it's a free newsletter, free report, news release, white paper, invitation, survey results, or research report on subjects that interest your subscriber.

DIRECT MAIL

To use direct mail effectively you have to ensure that the information is up-to-date and accurate. Pinpoint exactly who you're sending the mail to and why. Then you must plan the mail campaign considering the number of mail outs, whose on the list, how you are going to respond to enquiries, and what follow-up procedure you will use to gain the maximum results.

The mail out should be a personal letter that's no more than one page for the first contact. Then send a one-page brochure (full sales presentation in print) featuring all the benefits of what you want to achieve.

There is a strict process when following up on leads that eventually will go into the LNP. Go to "follow-up or close-up business" to find out more at http://www.commandobusiness.com/follow_up.php.

Referrals (for sales growth)

When you have made a sale, the process does not end. It just begins. There is a very valuable resource here to gain leads in the form of referrals. However, gaining referrals is not an easy thing to do. It takes great skill and effort from any sper or MOGUL.

The art of gaining referrals can be learned by going to "Getting the Best Referrals" at http://www.telcoblue.com.au/ecourse/modules/eCourse_Training_Module_9.pdf.

A simple way to gain referrals without a lot of effort is by asking the customer a few questions:

1. Mr. __(name)__, would you refer me and my product to others?

2. Would you refer people to me that you know who would benefit from my services?

If the customer responds negatively, simply ask them what you can do to gain his or her trust so that they would refer people to you. Then make sure they are reentered into your LNP to build the relationship for future referrals.

THE LEAD-GENERATING SYSTEM (THE FIRST SHEET) IS LISTED BELOW.

	Category	What	Month 1	Month 2	Month 3	Month 4
1	PUBLIC RELATIONS					
	Editorials	News				
	Magazines	Adverts				
	Newspapers	Comments/ reviews				
	Press Releases	News-changes				
	Radio	Advertising				
	Television	Campaigns				
	Article Placement	Various				
	eZine directories	White papers				
	Websites	Reprints				
		How-to books				
		eBooks				
2	DIRECT CONTACT					
	MAIL					
	Letter to individuals	Postcards				
	Letter to centres of influences	Personal letter				
		Newsletters				

(continued on next page)

	Category	What	Month 1	Month 2	Month 3	Month 4
	Cold Call					
	Face-to-Face	Phone calls				
		Door-knocking				
	Brochure	Letterbox drop				
	Promotions	Business door drop				
3	WEB BASE					
	Landing page	Email tips and bits				
	Blog					
	RSS					
4	BRANDING					
	Associations	Newsletters				
	Groups	Advertising				
	Professional organizations	Public speaking				
	Newspapers	Advertising in theirs				
	Newsletters	Helping them with yours				

	Category	What	Month 1	Month 2	Month 3	Month 4
5	EVENTS					
	Seminars	Attend or promote				
	Sales	Attend or promote				
	Business topics	Attend or promote				
	Trade shows	Attend or promote				
	General Public	Attend or promote				
	Business	Attend or promote				
	Trade	Attend or promote				
	Professional	Attend or promote				

This is only a base template. Build upon it using marketing channels that are appropriate for your specific industry. Adapt it to the particulars of your enterprise and the opportunities within your specific community.

Lead Nurturing Plan (LNP)

This is designed to register the contacts that may not be ready for you to market to them yet. With careful nurturing, they may be ready in a few months. A system of emails, letters, and/or visits will develop the lead into a qualified lead.

The goal of lead nurturing is to convert enquiries into qualified leads that will eventually purchase or be discarded as a potential customer in the sales process. Over time, the LNP builds a good relationship and trust with the lead. In other words, it is a system of follow-up on every enquiry with the hope of turning it into a sale.

As described in the Crab Pot section, all enquiries come into the opening of the pot and go through a process of being captured and eventually the lead may end up as a customer. So the name of the game is capturing as many names, enquiries, and contacts as possible. Build the relationship to a high level by turning that lead into a friend and customer. There are a number of benefits for you.

The new lead will have a certain amount of fear when being sold anything. I have covered many of the reasons that a customer may be uncertain about you or your product. Here are a few of those I have not covered.

The customer may be thinking about:

1. Is there a better and cheaper service?

2. Will it do exactly what the salesperson promises?

3. Do I really need this?

4. Is the backup service going to match my requirements?

In fact, a great LNP brings these concerns to the fore and answers them in detail before the customer brings them up. Anticipate these questions as if the customer or lead asked them him or herself.

Lead nurturing is all about building trust and removing the negative concerns in the customer's mind. The LNP must anticipate these concerns and cover them to the customer's satisfaction. If successful, the lead will say to themselves, "I want to do business with this person or company."

To be successful, the LNP must include continued follow-up with phone, email, and letters. Done correctly, you will never have to sell on price again.

Rather, it will be based on the virtues of your product and what it means to your customer.

Email Nurturing

As I mentioned before, email is the most readily accessible medium for lead generation. However, more than that, emails are most valued in the LNP. An email should follow any phone call with more information (see templates for email follow-up reasons).

If the "subscriber's box" promises information about a free newsletter, free report, news release, white paper, invitation, survey results, or a research report, your supporting emails must back up the promised information with relevant information.

Valuable content is what will interest the prospect. The purpose is to build a relationship of trust and value with your subscriber. The material that you offer must be relevant and perceived as full of interesting and worthwhile content.

Auto Responders Templates

The MOGUL must have the LNP established and ready to go. MOGULs use templates or a series of ready-made emails with information that is relevant to the topic in the subscriber box. Here are a few suggestions for the purpose of your email series:

1. Warm welcome to the education and benefits they will receive.

2. Enticing them to request more information about a subject that interests them.

3. Invitations to special events and competitions.

4. Ways in which they can improve their business.

5. Ask them to complete questionnaires and surveys.

6. Write to inform rather than sell.

Create different subscribers' boxes depending on the landing page topic they have chosen. Offer brochures, resource materials, or whatever else you can afford to give away for free provided it is perceived as valuable.

If a prospect has enquired and taken the time to subscribe to your box, you should reciprocate and develop a relationship with that individual. Here is a typical LNP plan for you to examine and individualise for your particular needs.

LEAD NURTURING PLAN (THE SECOND SHEET)

	CATEGORY	WHAT	Month 1	Month 2	Month 3	Month 4
1	PHONE CALLS					
	Build the relationship					
	Questionnaires					
	Referrals					
	Collect email addresses					
	Update information					
	Invitations					
	Qualifying					

2	DIRECT MAIL					
	Letters					
	Postcards					
	Newsletters					
	Brochures					
	White Papers					
	Invitations					
3	WEB BASE					
	Website					
	Blog					
	RSS					
4	Email					
	Newsletters					
	Links to and from sites					
	Invitations					
	Research					
5	EVENTS					
	Seminars					
	Trade shows					
	Product Nights					

Your database will assist you in managing the whole process. The follow-up, therefore, includes keeping records of contact and where the lead falls in the LNP. This is of paramount importance. For more on the art of following

MASTER STRATEGY 3

FUNDAMENTALS OF ACHIEVEMENT

CHAPTER 4 » All personal business achievement begins with knowing how to sell.

Learning how to sell is your foundation skill. Being able to sell your ideas to banks or businesses and being able to persuade people to give you what you want is essential to achievement. Don't mistake it. Skill at selling is the number one ingredient to success.

TIP: The wealthiest people I know owe their wealth to their selling skills, regardless of their station in life or their business.

The sales skills and techniques I'm going to show you are hardly traditional, and it's unlikely (unless you are already the leader in sales of your business) that you've ever heard or seen them previously.

These ideas may seem strange at first, but bear with me. We'll be looking at sales from a totally different point of view. It may not initially be obvious that our discussion has anything remotely to do with sales, but it will become clear the further we continue.

The Success Mindset

What is the biggest deterrent to success? Why do so many people fail? Here are just six ingredients you'll find valuable for improving your chances of success in life or business.

- Learn to control your reaction to rejection.

- Fight any tendencies you have of being A WORT ("Afraid of What Others Really Think").

- Learn to control your feelings of apprehension.

- Develop and maintain a good attitude.

- Learn a skilled technique.

- Set goals.

Obviously, there are other aspects of running a successful business. These six ingredients specifically involve the sales aspect of business.

While it's very important to achieve success, it's just as important that it's done correctly. When one's success has taken all six ingredients into account, it's solid and long-lasting. All six are necessary components.

Rejection

I believe there are two basic types of rejection sufferers. First, and by far the most common, are those who fear it. The second type of sufferers are those who do not actually fear rejection, but are just sick of it.

Hearing no all the time can be very discouraging to all of us. This is especially true if one doesn't quickly get what one wants. But why are some people more affected by rejection than others? Can those who fear rejection learn to gain more control over their fear? I have seen many people take all the right steps, set goals, work hard, yet still fail because they are paralyzed by their fear of rejection. There's no doubt about it; it's a force to be reckoned with.

It is really a matter of how each person perceives the events he or she faces. If we all were made powerless by rejection, real or perceived, then we would all be equally affected by it. But we know this isn't the case. Some people even view rejection as a welcome thing!

TIP: It's the things that one tells oneself about events that will govern how he or she reacts to them.

We Are What We Think We Are

The internal dialogue of successful people is completely different than that of a low achiever. The latter talk to themselves, too, but they have different purposes and results. For those overly sensitive to rejection, inappropriate self-talk leads to feelings of rejection.

So why do people respond differently to similar events or challenges? Because the self-talk each individual makes about the event is different.

That's something you should never forget. Your feelings are largely created by your thoughts. If you are a person who is easily hurt and suffers a lot of stress, depression, anxiety, or hostility, it's not the conditions of your life that are the cause.

NEGATIVE RESPONSES

Being able to identify a negative or irrational pattern of self-talk is not enough. You have to overcome an inappropriate negative response. Just identifying that you're saying the wrong thing will not help you fix anything.

There are plenty of medical stories that demonstrates people can think themselves into being sick. Yet knowing that negative thinking can make one physically sick rarely provides enough motivation to push individuals towards making the necessary changes. If someone wishes to overcome an inappropriate reaction what should they do?

TIP: Once you've trained yourself to recognize your negative thought responses, learn to intervene and turn it into positive self-talk.

I've trained myself to recognize and put out of my mind thoughts that will not enhance my self-image. You can too! This always sounds unachievable when we take those early, tentative steps towards a goal. But remember, so many of us were in your shoes and were able to attain our goals. Like any skill, all it takes is constant practice. Nothing worthwhile comes without effort, and this is one of the most worthwhile skills you'll ever master.

THE SHARP BLADE OF LOGIC

When you dispute your negative thoughts, you question them. You challenge them to withstand the strict judgment of logic.

TIP: By constantly and vigorously disputing your negative thought responses, you'll realize how foolish and self-defeating they are. Soon, you will become less affected by them.

I really can't stress this enough. It's got to be constant, and it has to be vigorous. This doesn't just apply on your good days. You've got to keep it up on those days when you're at your weakest. This means even when you haven't gotten enough sleep, you're moody, or you're under the weather. Those are the times when you'll make the biggest headway in the battle.

The ABCs of Success in Business

Let's examine some structural fundamentals of doing business.

Business is simple in concept but difficult in execution. To make money in your business you must make certain things happen in a specific order. I call these steps:

Attract people.

Bag and capture customers.

Collect cash and make profit.

TIP: These aren't tangible. It's more of a mindset. You accomplish these fundamentals using your brains, not your brawn.

Yes, you will have to use your brains, but this isn't going to end with an intellectual process. Take time to think about how best to implement your steps to achieve the ABCs. Once you've done that, figure out the systems to accomplish these using automated processes. How is that done?

- First, identify a problem that exists within your market.

- Find a way to solve that problem for the customer with your product or service that will be simple and easy.

- Make more money than the solution costs to implement.

Traps That Lead to Failure

Most astute business-minded people know these basic rules. Why do so many fail then?

TIP: People fail because they don't do what high achievers do.

And why not? To examine this, we could use a number of different scenarios in various occupations from business or personal life. Relate the information to your specific situation. For this example let's look at a typical industry where commissioned sales play a large part in the remuneration for employees.

It is my experience that 70 percent of those entering the commission selling industry will quit within the first year. For example, if one hundred people are accepted into the industry in August, seventy of them will leave the position before the next August! That means, at any given time, over half of the salespeople are "newbies" with less than one year's experience!

True Sales Ability Is a Rare Skill

90 percent of those in commission selling achieve, at best, moderate success before they want out. That means less than one out of every ten recruits after the first year go on to become a moderate to high performer, or what I call those with the potential to be a true professional.

No wonder so many of us don't like salespeople. Most don't know how to sell simply because they lack the experience. That's why we find it such a pleasure to be influenced by a truly professional salesperson.

It's imperative that a business achieve good results from everybody as soon as possible. Once someone has decided to leave sales, recovering or enhancing that person's performance is essentially a lost cause.

Discontentment

I've read that around 70 percent of those in the workforce are not content with their current job, and that those with a consistent salary are less likely to leave those jobs. When it comes to those earning commission, it's a whole different ballgame. Without the security of a regular paycheck, the discontented or discouraged salesperson is much more likely to pack it in.

That's why both consumers and businesspeople are constantly plagued with inexperienced salespeople.

THOUGHT: The fact that so many wage earners stick with jobs that they dislike creates a whole set of different problems.

Ask yourself, would a person work effectively in a business he or she doesn't like? Maybe in the short-term or until they found another job. But at any given time, the world is dealing with the costly inefficiency of discontented wage earners.

Remember my question about why people who aren't successful don't simply do the same things that successful people do? Consider the examples above before you hire people, either in commissioned sales or as wage earners. I think it's easy to see that a lot of managers and owners are not using the same criteria for hiring and retaining staff that successful managers and owners are.

TIP: Feeling discouraged is not a problem. It is the symptom of a problem.

Business Responsibilities

Many make the mistake of believing that the traits and qualities of successful people in one business will translate to success in another business. Hogwash!

It doesn't matter how successful someone is in another walk of life. If they are like most people in the population and overly sensitive to rejection, they are unlikely to make it big on their own.

When the fear of rejection takes hold, it distracts from the task at hand. It results in emotional reactions to real or imagined personal attacks. In short, it negatively affects work productivity. It can even effect the morale of those dealing with the emotional outbursts of the overly sensitive individual.

Let me come back to the story of AJ. Since starting with me, we had the usual trials of working through his apprenticeship. However, from time to time over the next two years or so, AJ would always be short of money. I couldn't understand why. (I learned later he had an addiction to horse racing, and he also gave into other weaknesses in his character.)

We were close business associates and had developed a close friendship. We spent a lot of time together going through strategies, planning, and sales training courses. Even though he was earning around $20,000 a month, I gave him huge amounts of money numerous times to help him survive his bad gambling debts.

Whenever this need for money occurred (evidenced by his negative attitude and behaviour), he displayed depression along with comments of insecurity. He would accuse me of treating him unjustly, and at times he would tell others about how he disliked being obligated to me. The warning bells rang loudly. I knew it was time for more assistance. I had to help him build his self-esteem through affirmations.

The solution every time was to take him under my wing, go through the personal development techniques again, and practice the rudiments of the action plan. His attitude would change as if overnight. But it was hard for him to concentrate on the good in his life rather than all the negatives. Without his personal development plan, he was a lost soul.

It's a slack manager indeed who will put up with that. Unfortunately, many do. Don't be one of them. There'll be more about AJ later.

Business

TIP: When starting in business, one must be organized.

If you go into business, you must treat it as a business from day one. You will need to seek your accountant's advice, you'll need sound legal guidance, and you must be familiar with all relevant local and national legislation.

TIP: Even if you are starting a home business, make sure you keep accurate records and accounts for your annual tax return.

If you treat your business as a hobby or a part-time job, that is exactly what it will remain. You'll never advance any further. Don't make that mistake as so many before you. Get yourself professional advice from the very start.

You need to be able to grasp your company's financial position at any time. You must know the areas that are most profitable and where you spend the most cash and time.

How to Pick Professionals

TIP: When you seek professional advice, remember that all accountants are not made equal!

I shouldn't have to warn you about bad accountants. The financial news is filled with stories of companies or businesspeople who have lost all or most of their fortunes because of crooked or sloppy accounting. Also avoid the "creative" accountant: the so-called professional who says you can do this or that to reduce your tax substantially. There's a bomb waiting to go off.

If your tax department or body gets the slightest indication you are not being fair and reasonable in your claims, they're entitled to go through your entire business with a fine-tooth comb. Again, you read of this happening everyday. So why do people still make those mistakes?

TIP: There is a tremendous amount of business advice available through government departments. It's usually free or for a nominal fee. Many banks and local authorities also offer guidance.

If the logistics of your business allow, you should dedicate an area in your home specifically for your venture. It doesn't need to be a large area, but it needs to be enough to comfortably and realistically operate in a businesslike manner.

Home Office

Ideally, the office should have a telephone. A kitchen, for instance, is likely to offer distractions and noises that negatively affect the professional nature of your business calls.

Spend a bit of money for professional letterhead paper, and print up some tasteful business cards. Make sure you get quotes for all the work related to your start-up so you don't waste money on unpleasant "surprises."

It is also wise, regardless of how experienced you are, to find a mentor whose wisdom and abilities can guide you. Bear in mind this isn't a person you should strive to impress. You need to communicate your frustrations, shortcomings, mistakes, and fears to your mentor. That's the only way he or she will be able to offer you valuable counsel.

Is It Just Too Good to Be True?

You hear it everywhere you go: buyer beware. Fear of being scammed has been hammered into our consciousness. And you know what? It's all true!

Don't fall into traps and get stung. I've had friends venture into get-rich-quick schemes and pie-in-the-sky promises of high-interest returns on investments. All have been burned; none of them were spared. These are nothing new. They're just this year's model. They're a new twist or a different facade on the same improbable scams. Yet year after year, people fall victim.

Anyone Can Call Himself an Expert

Our culture is awash with "experts," "specialists," and "think tanks" peddling their expertise to anyone willing to buy.

TIP: If you need a diamond ring appraised, don't go to a bricklayer.

Similarly, when it comes to advice on how to grow your income, don't trust their advice if they can't *prove* they are an expert in the field. And if they never achieved in the past what they are now promoting, I have to wonder why anyone would even listen to their advice.

These people are smooth and very convincing. But they have no "secrets." Chances are, the only wealth they've ever known has come from selling repackaged information to people unwilling to look beneath the surface.

Sorting through the Rubble to Find the Diamonds

I don't know about you, but I'm constantly on the lookout for scams and scammers. And I'm wary of anyone who offers promos that are too good to be true. I want definitive answers without the filler. I want a promoter to spell out "here is how to make a difference," and that's it. The mere thought of reading a thousand pages of marketing palaver makes me sick.

Honestly, how can anyone think these people are going to tell them anything useful? At best it'll be the same info you already knew or could find out yourself with little effort.

And when it comes to "this year's model," making money on the Internet, I've yet to see a simple but accurate step-by-step guide that is sure to work at a reasonable price. Often they want money up front before you can evaluate the product to see if it will work for you.

I'm not saying there aren't legitimate experts or authors out there with some great money-making schemes. But the question is, which ones are they? And how do you identify them when there are so many products and gurus out there?

TIP: The best advice I can give to someone who wants to start up an Internet business is to get a coach, get a coach, get a coach!

TIP: If you want to get ahead, be prepared for a lot of hard work. Don't trust those who tell you there's an easy way out.

SUCCESS SMILES ON THE ORGANIZED

The potential of a great business grows out of the structure you use to set it up. There are many structures to operate under, but the best for most people is a Propriety Limited company. (This generally limits your liability to the company assets.) However, your accountant may suggest something different for your specific situation, and it's imperative that you consult with one before launching your venture.

There are many expenses incurred in running any business. You may be able to claim such expenditures as:

- Petrol for driving to your prospect's houses or to meetings to operate the business. You may also be entitled to a portion of servicing and depreciation costs of your vehicle.

- Costs associated with running your office including heating, lighting, furnishing, and cleaning. More potential claims are postage, renewal fees, bank charges, advertising, your telephone bill, business aids, tapes, books, stationery, sales literature, tickets for seminars, and products used for demonstration purposes.

As you can see, keeping accurate accounts of your business is time well spent!

The Elusive Profits

If you are not careful, you may find that your profits are eaten up by extra costs. It is easy to become disillusioned and start to think you may never break even.

Many people have given up on their business because of this type of financial stress. But usually all that was missing was a little bit of planning and common sense.

TIP: Use planning sheets, time planners, and budget sheets to help you organize your business.

Manage Time—Like Your Life Depends on It!

Set yourself a schedule, and keep to it. Time is very precious, especially when you are building a business around the demands of a full-time job.

Be very strict with yourself, and be polite and assertive with others when it comes to your focus and time. As Benjamin Franklin said, "Time is money." Spend that precious commodity wisely and on productive tasks.

TIP: The best way to stay on task is to ask yourself, "am I spending my time wisely?"

Ask yourself, what is the course I will follow next year to achieve what I want? Like the captain of a ship, you must plot your course so you can reach your destination by the most direct route.

You have to check your progress along the way and, if required, make adjustments to your course. In charting your course, you need to follow these four steps:

1. DETERMINE THE AMOUNT OF INCOME YOU WOULD LIKE TO HAVE DURING THE YEAR.

2. WHEN YOU KNOW HOW MUCH YOU MUST EARN, TRANSLATE DOLLARS INTO ACTIVITY.

   For example, in order to earn money as a businessperson or sales representative, you must seek prospects, make presentations to those prospects, secure applications, and send them in for processing. Figure out how many presentations you will need to achieve your required income.

   How many appointments will you need to secure that many presentations? How many phone calls would you need to secure that many appointments?

TIP: Your annual objectives should be translated into monthly and weekly target objects.

---

3. CREATE A BUDGET AND ORGANIZE YOUR RECORD KEEPING.

If you think your quotas are too huge for the year, break them down to manageable weekly or hourly targets and achieve this each day.

4. YOU MUST CREATE A RECORD KEEPING PROCEDURE THAT WILL TRACK YOUR PROGRESS ACCURATELY.

A major challenge of keeping to a schedule of activities and self-improvement is knowing exactly what you have accomplished each day.

Keep track of your progress on steps two and three above as well as your year's objectives. While you will be able to make up deficits periodically, you cannot afford to fall so far behind that it would be impossible to catch up.

TIP: We all have to determine how much our time is worth. How much are we worth on an hourly, daily, or yearly basis?

Calculating the dollar value of your time is easy. If you work full time, divide your present annual income by two thousand, and that's how much each of your hours is worth. If you work fewer hours, divide your income by that number.

For example, if your annual earnings are $40,000, then each hour is worth twenty dollars. That is based on 250, eight-hour working days in a year. How does this help you? It allows you to place a value on the cost of your spare time as well.

Let's assume the average person watches three hours of television per night, or twenty-one hours a week (approximately twenty hours for easy calculation). If that person is earning $40,000 a year, the cost of that time watching TV is $400 per week or $20,000 a year!

Imagine what you could earn if you started a part-time business by working those three hours each night instead of watching television.

Ask yourself these simple questions:

- Do you spend very much time on activities that are not moving you closer to your goals?

- Are you using your spare time effectively?

Big Money Earners

We have just examined how much a worker earns per hour based on a $40,000 a year income. The CEO of that worker's company could earn as much as two million dollars a year. Why does one earn $40,000 and another earns fifty times that amount?

Leverage: The Power Tool of the Rich

Time is even more precious than money.

This is one of the secrets of wealth that the rich keep to themselves. It is called "leverage." When a worker gives his or her time in exchange for dollars, his or her income grows by the units of time given to the business. One unit of time equals one unit of money.

What the worker earns is totally based on his or her own effort. CEOs, on the other hand, leverage their time through the employees. Instead of only being paid for 100 percent of their own efforts, they also make a percentage of all the employees' efforts.

Learn from the advice of the world's richest. J. Paul Getty once said, "I'd rather earn 1 percent of one hundred people's efforts than 100 percent of my own effort."

TIP: If you can find a way to earn a few cents from the efforts of a lot of people, you have the secret of the rich.

That is the magic of leverage, and it is very powerful. Let me give you another example of its effectiveness. Each person has twenty-four hours in a day. And this is usually broken up into three sections:

1. Eight hours work

2. Eight hours sleep, and

3. Eight hours leisure or family time

Let's calculate the maximum potential income an individual could earn if he or she devoted all available, waking hours to work.

We would have eight hours work plus the eight hours in section three above, which is sixteen hours a day available for generating income. Multiply sixteen hours per day by seven days, and you have a maximum of 112 hours available to every person to earn an income. Let's examine the following example:

EXAMPLE 1:

8 hours work + 8 hours other = 16 hours per day available to earn an income.

16 hours x 7 days   = 112 hours maximum available per week to earn an income.

$20 x 112 hours   = $2240 maximum pay per week

$2240 x 52 weeks   = $116,480 maximum earning potential per annum

You may say 112 hours per week is unreasonable, and you're right. Most people would never last the distance.

EXAMPLE 2:

As discussed above, there are twenty-four hours available to everyone. Let's assume you don't want to work constantly, like in the above example. Instead, you take J. P. Getty's advice, and you hire 800 part-time people to work for just one hour each day. Now there are 800 hours that are being worked five days a week.

800 people x 1 hour = 800 hours per day

800 hours x 5 days = 4000 hours per week

$1 x 4000 hours = $4,000 per week

$4,000 x 52 weeks = $208,000 per annum earning

That's 4000 hours per week instead of 112, which is the maximum you can do on your own. Let's say for that 4000 hours you only received one dollar per hour from the efforts of others, which is $4000 per week.

Multiply $4000 per week by fifty-two weeks, and that gives you an income of $208,000 a year. That is not counting the hours you may work yourself.

You may say this example is unrealistic.

EXAMPLE 3:

Say you have one hundred part-time people working one hour a day for you. That would be one hundred hours per day. Multiply that by five days, which makes five hundred hours a week instead of the original 112 hours if you worked alone.

If you receive a dollar for every hour from each of these individuals, you'll earn $500 a week. Multiply $500 by fifty-two weeks, and that gives you

$26,000 for the year. That is still without you working, and your people only giving you one dollar for one hour of work each week.

That is the power of leverage.

Simple Things

Sometimes people don't look at a situation from a commercial point of view. Let's say I have an income of one million dollars a year. On a forty-hour workweek for fifty-two weeks of the year, that comes out to approximately $500 an hour.

Sometimes during my day, though, I'm not always effectively making $500 an hour. However, I may be planning things that will produce that over a twelve-month period. For example, when I ring up to order photocopy paper, it might be a thousand dollars worth. I may feel as though I am being overcharged by $150.

Unless it's easy, I'll not negotiate this amount of money. It is only going to hurt my efforts to earn my $500 an hour elsewhere. It could take me fifteen to twenty minutes to save a lousy twenty bucks or so.

And where is the benefit in that? If it diverts me from my primary objective—to produce $500 an hour—why would I waste my ability to earn that income just to save ten, fifteen, or twenty dollars?

TIP: It's wise to always consider how much time a task will take. It's also wise to determine how long fixing a problem is likely to take.

If it takes me half an hour, it had better save me $250 at the very least. Wealthy people tend not to waste time on mundane things unless it's for pleasure.

Let me explain. While it is important not to be ripped off and to negotiate a good price on everything, the principle here is not to get sidetracked and lose focus of what's important.

Some people will just never understand this and will argue for days over a twenty dollar savings. That is not the way a practical, wealthy person would do it.

Putting It All Together

In the upcoming chapters, you'll learn how to take what you've learned and put it into practice. This information will help you plan and organize your steps and start your business venture without encountering pitfalls.

Bad luck will be for others. *Not* you. Others will admire you as someone who has the golden touch.

MASTER STRATEGY 4

REQUISITES TO AVOID FINANCIAL DISAPPOINTMENT

CHAPTER 5 » Make no bones about it. To make big changes to your life and business, it's going to take a lot of commitment. In the beginning, I could barely scrape enough to keep us fed, but I was able to build my business to a value of $140 million in eighteen months and enjoy more than $80,000 per month in income.

As I look back and analyse what worked and didn't work for me, I realize that I can credit the bulk of my success to two major steps.

TIP: Learn how to sell.

Becoming aware of the basic laws of life and learning how to adapt them was difficult. Mastering the art of selling involves many hours of learning how to persuade others.

Easier said than done, right? Just how do you go about becoming proficient in selling ideas to others?

My "NEXT" Philosophy

We're going to return to a concept I introduced you to earlier—my "NEXT" Philosophy. Specifically, we'll be looking at two crucial components. If you learn these concepts, you won't have a problem with your personal and business growth.

1. MOVE PAST THOSE NEGATIVES TO THE NEXT EVENT

There's only one way to counteract your negative responses. You've got to neutralize it by moving on to the NEXT event. Make this part of your daily life, and make the word "next" part of your mental vocabulary.

Sure, the prospect you're talking to is usually more important than the next call you're planning to make. But there comes a time when it is no longer in your best interest to pursue a prospect that is not likely to budge. Winning isn't the goal—making money is. NEXT simply means you do your best with every prospect or client, but if things don't go your way, then you have to move on.

High achievers don't just make use of the NEXT concept when they've been rejected. It's also the first thought after enjoying a successful call. It becomes a life philosophy that propels them forward and guarantees them continuing success.

2. DON'T WAIT FOR PEOPLE TO COME TO YOU. YOU GO TO THEM.

At one time, I worked for Combined Insurance Company of America (CICA). When they employed me, they encouraged me to follow this affirmation: "If it's human and it moves, present to it."

Become a contacting machine. I was taught to sell to as many people as I could with persistence and belief in my cause.

In order to close more deals, you need experience. This requires practice, especially in the early days of building your business. By contacting as many people as possible, you improve your chances of closing more deals. But you also have more opportunity to develop skill and experience in knowing what works.

TIP: If you feel low and lose interest, remember that action creates motivation. Increase the number of people you see, and you'll feel better.

High achievers don't only attribute their success to goals, self-esteem, and positive attitude. Most would say it is control over one's apprehension that plays the most important role.

But I have found that only 10 percent of businesspeople have this attitude. The other 90 percent are affected to such a high degree by their fear of rejection that it interferes with their ability to make the sale. Unless the sale is handed to them on a silver platter, they simply give up too easily to win over the prospect.

TIP: One's self-talk and beliefs on how to handle a situation will govern the outcome of events.

If you find it too hard to counter the prospect's reluctance, or if you're too scared, you've lost the sale. Any type of self-talk that is self-defeating will nearly always lose you the sale.

Attitude and Fear

"Attitude" is your key to making powerful change. Many people teach selling and prospecting techniques. But no amount of technique can change a person's negative attitude. Attitude is the leader; technique follows.

TIP: The businessperson's most valuable and important quality is the ability to control his or her apprehension.

The ability to control fear is the high achiever's greatest trait. Rarely do training programs deal with the subject of fear in enough detail. I find that the reason it is avoided is just bringing up the subject causes apprehension, so many authors and business coaches avoid it like they would any other negative subject matter.

But positive thinking doesn't mean you close your eyes to reality. Remember negative but optimistic views are part of a successful strategy. Delusion makes it nearly impossible to solve problems.

"Conventional Wisdom" Can Be Wrong!

You have no doubt heard the cliché, "He could have been a great salesperson but didn't know how to handle the no's."

This thought has long been popular, but it is not entirely correct. Let's change it so its advice is more valuable: "He could have been a great salesperson if he learned to control his self-talk and feelings of rejection."

When people are not performing, we often bombard them with goal setting techniques. We expose them to motivational material, tell them to be optimistic, tell them to think positively, and lecture them on the importance of positive self-esteem and self-discipline. The list is endless.

We stereotype them and rarely take time to identify if they actually are negative thinkers. We tend to massage the head when the problems are in the neck. We may be wasting their time focusing their attention on problems that don't exist. We could be diverting them from fixing the real issues they need to address.

TIP: If the wrong thinking doesn't go away, income and success will.

There is another old cliché that says: "Do the thing you fear the most, and the death of fear is certain." Unfortunately, this is not entirely correct either. In fact, if taken at face value, this piece of "conventional wisdom" can sometimes cause more harm than good.

Let's take rejection as an example. The cliché implies that if you expose yourself to rejection, you will become less fearful of it. This is wrong. If you expose yourself to rejection, and your thoughts regarding rejection are that of a negative self-talker, the intensity of your emotional reaction will validate your original fear. Even worse, your reaction will likely grow with each encounter until you're so fearful you may even stop selling.

"Conventional wisdom" indeed!

Instead, let's consider the approach of the high achiever. Exposure to rejection leads to a reaction that the high achiever sets out to control. Skilled as he or she is in the right sort of self-talk, any negative self-talk is immediately controlled before damage can occur.

Can you see how another popular cliché, "every no brings you closer to a yes," can be quickly turned into "every no brings you closer to a more intense rejection problem?"

Do the thing you fear most, but make sure you're well on your way to mastering the right sort of self-talk. As long as you maintain appropriate thinking patterns, fear will be unable to disrupt your ambitions.

The Beauty of the Averages Game

The truth at the core of the Averages Game is what keeps the high achiever persevering. I'm not talking about sales ratios for the sake of ratios. I'm not advocating cold calling examples, such as if you knock on ten doors and you get one sale, knock on twenty to make two sales.

In this book I have already outlined many alternatives to cold calling. Although I am going to use a door-knocking example here to illustrate the power of ratios, keep an open mind to get past the ratios idea alone and see the real benefit from the understanding of them.

It's hard to fathom how so many people go through life without ever learning to make use of this valuable strategy.

TIP: If you take a particular action and get a result, that result will remain constant or improve each time you repeat that same action.

For example, many years ago, I sold telecommunications services to businesses door-to-door. I found that for every fourteen doors I knocked on, I managed to complete my sales presentation from start to finish four times. Out of the four presentations, I would close two sales.

Therefore, if I knocked at the doors of forty-two businesses a day, I'd write six sales a day. That meant $600 commission for my own pocket!

Knocking on that many doors in a day was entirely possible, but not if I dillydallied or wasted time. This is where my NEXT philosophy came into play. It didn't matter if someone wasn't home, didn't like me, was rude, or gave me a hard time. All that mattered was to move to the NEXT door. It was a powerful motivation.

TIP: Focus on the bounty of the averages. Coupled with proper self-talk, rejection and apprehension is less likely to affect you.

Whatever part of prospecting or marketing you're involved in, whether door-knocking, telephone calling, or mailing letters, you will gain plenty of data to develop your success ratio formula.

Use this ratio to set your sales goals for the day, week, and/or month. If you wish to close more sales, you can tweak this ratio by increasing the number you contact or improving your presentation. In either case, you now have real numbers that can help you plan your approach, monitor your improvement, and motivate you to keep at it.

The 80/20 Rule

What if I told you 80 percent of people in sales (or any business) produce 20 percent of the business, and 80 percent of the business that is produced comes from 20 percent of the customers. Would that surprise you?

It's all about ratios. I'm not talking about the number of calls necessary to secure a given number of appointments. What I'm talking about is the ratio between the number of calls and that given number of appointments.

Not every appointment will turn into a sale, even for the best salespeople. The reality is that very few will.

Unfortunately, that's just the beginning of the bad news. One out of every five cold prospects that make an appointment to meet with you won't even be there when you show up. Of the remaining four, you'll discover that one won't be a good match with your services. Three will listen to you, and one will buy if you've done your job properly.

These are the averages for five cold appointments. But this does not mean it has to be your average.

I know someone who door-knocked 120 houses and wrote up fifty-seven sales in one day, which earned him a total of $651 in commissions. Once you know what your ratios are, you will know your averages.

Let's look at what I've said here. I've given you the winning numbers, the formula for never failing in sales. I know this is worth a million dollars to someone who will pick up on it.

Let me say it another way. If you recall my previous example, I knocked on forty-two doors to write six sales.

There was a total of twenty-one people actually seen and ten presented to. Six bought from me. Therefore, my ratios out of every ten were:

Doors knocked	10
People seen	5
Completed presentations	2.5
Sales from presentations	1.5

Making the Averages Work for Me

I understood what the averages were telling me. All I had to do to make 1.5 sales a day was knock on ten doors. If I wanted to make six sales a day I'd have to knock on forty-two doors.

Suddenly doors were looking pretty valuable to me. Every one I went through was worth $15.50 ($651 divided by 42 doors), whether I made a sale or not!

Improving Your Averages

Of course, if you can improve on your average, you'll earn more money with less work. Who's going to turn that down?

But how do you go about bettering the averages? By being a good prospector. For example, a good prospector only selects those who aren't going to pull appointment no-shows. They know that prospects are less likely to cancel if the appointment has been confirmed.

In other words, top prospectors are screening their pool of prospects and only selecting those who are "qualified."

How to Become a Master Lead Generator (Prospector)

This is where the power of ratios comes into play. The real power is in the self-generating of leads and sales, rather than cold calling, that you benefit most. When prospecting, only make appointments with those you've already determined are qualified. By qualified I mean someone who does not harbour the most common reasons for not buying. These will be specific, of course, to your line of business and your product.

A master prospector is someone who knows the most common reasons for prospects not buying. When prospecting, they will check to see if these reasons are present in those they plan to contact.

TIP: Master prospector's fail less often than master salespeople.

Following this simple principle will allow you to better focus your time and efforts. It sounds pretty basic and a bit obvious, doesn't it? But you'd be surprised at the number of salespeople who never seem to realize this. And knowing this could make the difference between success and failure in selling.

In fact, I believe that someone who may not have a lot of selling skill but is confident and doesn't have an apprehensive attitude will be more successful than a more experienced salesperson who lacks prospecting skills and the right kind of self-talk.

TIP: Master prospectors only make appointments with those they feel are worthy of their time and energy.

A qualified prospect is capable of and has the authority to buy from you, appears interested in buying from you, and is motivated to see a deal between you go through.

Let's say you go out cold prospecting and get fifteen appointments. Naturally, you don't know yet how many will end up being qualified or not. On average, of the fifteen, three will miss or cancel your appointment, three won't be qualified, and you'll present your pitch to the remaining nine. According to averages, three of those nine will buy from you.

While that may make you a decent enough prospector in terms of activity, I would have to say because of your low sales results to effort that you're not a good prospector with those averages. It would only be good prospecting if around ten or more of these appointments became sales.

You may think the number of prospects sold depends on one's selling skills. This is not necessarily so.

TIP: I believe the number that is sold depends more on the quality of the prospect than the salesperson's selling skills.

If you mastered the art of prospecting and only presented to qualified prospects, you would have only called upon roughly one third of the original fifteen in the example above. That saves you time, which can be spent pursuing other qualified prospects.

The average salesperson in most industries probably wastes around eight or more hours a week on unqualified prospects. No wonder so many salespeople are not successful.

TIP: You know you've got it mastered when you no longer have to make so many appointments to meet your sales goals.

"I can teach you how to successfully sell to seven out of every ten prospects," I tell the flabbergasted people in my sales training courses. They stare back at me in disbelief, especially any that have insurance sales in their background.

I can understand if they're skeptical at first. Back when I was first learning sales, I constantly found myself presenting to prospects that would listen to me attentively then never sign on the dotted line. I thought there just had to be a problem in my sales presentation.

This was a natural assumption to make, and most would conclude exactly the same thing. But when I investigated my situation further, I learned the failure was not within the selling process but in the prospecting. Despite agreeing to meet with me, too many of my prospects shared the most common reasons for not buying.

Most of us know high achievers who make a sale on nearly every presentation. We automatically assume they are great salespeople who have a perfect presentation, when in fact, their prospecting skills (selling to qualified prospects) are usually the reason for their success.

TIP: Time is wasted because prospects aren't qualified.

Just think how much time is wasted travelling back and forth to prospects who turn out to be unqualified. Let's say you took twenty minutes travelling to the prospect, five minutes to realize they were not suited, and another twenty minutes to get back to the office. That's forty-five minutes. What if you spent thirty minutes instead of the five minutes suggested before? Now you've jumped your wasted time to one hour and ten minutes!

Think for a minute how much you could achieve if the travel time and the time spent getting appointments for unqualified prospects was better used in the qualification process? Say eight hours a week was spent on gaining better prospects. How would that benefit you?

Learn to Offer

Are you more comfortable asking for something from someone or offering something to them? You're probably more comfortable offering than asking. Even the high achievers claim they would sooner offer than ask.

Would you rather have someone ask you for something or offer you something? If you are like most people, high achievers included, you would rather be offered something than be asked for something.

What does this tell us? If we're meeting with a prospect who is both willing and able to buy from us, then we're most likely offering our deal to him or her. But if we're meeting with a contact that may or may not be qualified, we're asking him or her to consider us and our product.

To be more comfortable with prospecting, we don't have to learn to ask. Rather, we have to learn to offer. You see, we've all been told that the skill of prospecting and selling is turning your prospect's no into a yes. We have been told we shouldn't believe the unqualified prospect until they have said no five times.

But all this is unnecessary if all your prospects are qualified.

The Killer Instinct

I was given an article titled "The Killer Instinct" when I was working for the National Mutual Insurance Company in the late '70s. It made me sit up and ponder here it is:

> There was a man filling out an application for life insurance. He came to the question about the cause of his father's death.
>
> His father had been hanged for treason. So after some thought he wrote, "He was taking part in a public ceremony, and the platform he stood on gave way."

If you asked most successful people to list the qualities a person needs in order to be a success in business, the list would likely look like this:

* The person must have good people skills.

* He must know his products.

* He must be a good prospector.

* He must be able to discipline himself.

* He must be a good business manager.

* He must study regularly.

* He must attend seminars.

* He must keep in contact with his clients.

* He must have a good, quality business.

* He must be socially mobile.

* He must possess a good grounding in commercial principles.

* He must have a supportive partner, a natural market, and a desire for success.

Of course, not all of these will be appropriate for our individual situations, but we all must possess some or all of these characteristics in varying degrees.

But the one crucial trait we all need in order to be a high achiever is what I call the "Killer Instinct."

I'm not talking about the level of aggression that makes someone punch another in the nose. I mean the kind of controlled aggression that motivates you to sink your teeth in and not let go. You could also call this determination. We all have this killer instinct; otherwise, we would not be successful.

It is my contention that the high achiever uses it more often and more effectively. For example, when handling the objection, "I'll think about it, and I will call you tomorrow," what would you do?

This is the perfect time for you to grit your teeth and put a "tiger in your tank." If you firmly believe that the client needs your product or service, and you are convinced that they can afford it, then for goodness sake, get in there fighting, boots and all. Don't just sit back under the delusion that this person really does want to think about it.

The facts say differently. People are busy, and considering your proposal is likely to get relegated to the back burner. Get aggressive. Let them know by your actions and tone of voice that you expect them to do their duty and follow your recommendation. Let them say, "This person's serious. They're concerned about me!" And isn't that what it's all about?

You are serious, and you are concerned. If you treat it lightly, they'll treat it lightly, too. Let them know they should be seriously considering this concept. I've heard the excuses. "I don't want them to think I'm pushy," or "That's just not my style."

What you're likely communicating is the message that you don't believe in what you are doing. Are you afraid of losing the sale if you get aggressive? What sale? At this stage, you have none.

Don't wait to "put that tiger in your tank" until the client is already saying no. Your tiger should be continually on the prowl throughout the sale presentation, revealing itself occasionally in the words you use and the enthusiasm you display.

An awful lot of men and women who played sports do well in our industry, and I believe a contributing factor is the competitive aggressiveness they have learned.

Conclusion

Now that you are armed with this information and want to be a high achiever, make sure you take all the steps I outlined. You must study, prospect, and train.

Remember, as well as sharpening your skills, you must be aggressive in the way you apply them. But one final note of caution. I must strongly stress that I am not advocating you blindly attack everyone you see with your own particular brand of ebullience.

You must first be sure that the person you are dealing with has a need, the ability to pay, and the moral fiber to use your service or goods.

For those of you who may have some skills in selling, if you want a more advanced eCourse in selling go to www.TelcoBlue.com.au and join up. As a member, you can log into the training course.

You will have to relate the information in the course to your particular situation. It's their company sales course written specifically for their salespeople for their products. They do not sell it to the public. A major part of this course is the qualification process under the title of the "Big D."

The skills learned will enhance your life both personally and financially, and it will create more harmonious relationships.

THE NUTS & BOLTS
OF STAFFING, GOALS, AND PLAN OF ACTION

SPECIAL NUTS & BOLTS SECTION B

 Funding the Growth

CREDIT CARDS AND CREDIT LINES

>> **THE TIME** to set up lines of credit is before you need it. That way, when your company needs capital to expand, or if you have an emergency, your solution has been prearranged.

Here are some options you should pursue:

- A chequebook facility backed by signature only.

- Chequebook facility backed by credit line.

- Credit cards limit increase.

- Apply for at least five more credit cards within one day (otherwise a new one every six months).

- Internet banking.

- A credit line.

- Extend an existing credit line with your present suppliers. Ask to go from thirty days to ninety days. If this isn't doable, build up your credit as far as you can.

These methods will provide access to many hundreds of thousands of dollars in case of an emergency. But managing this situation is paramount. Temptation has ruined many good businesspeople when they were faced with too much readily available cash. This money is not for joyriding. It is strictly for business.

For valuable hints on how to manage your company's credit, go to http://www.commandobusiness.com/financial_crisis_%20part_two.php. Ask yourself this question: Are you financially OK at the moment? Does your business need money urgently?

If your answer is no, you must do three things.

- Immediately secure at least three lines of credit using any of the methods identified above.

- Plan out how you will turn that cash into five times the original amount within twelve months.

- Arrange your affairs so that if you have a financial crisis you can use a round-robin system for a six-month period. For example, use one credit card to pay off a debt and use a second credit card to pay back the first credit card when due. This gives you time to set things right.

TIP: Preparation prevents poor planning.

 ## *The Biggest Mistakes I Made*

Financial Crises Will Happen. Will You Survive?

About a month or two after launching my business, I did some pro forma projections and concluded that my company had a huge potential for growth. This immediately put me outside my comfort zone. I sought the advice of the very best accountant I could find.

I presented my projections and my plans to the accountant. I discovered that I had to restructure my business for it to function in an orderly and profitable manner.

The result of that restructuring process meant that I was blessed with some tax breaks along the way. These weren't planned, but they became available because of the way we structured the business.

Knowing what I know about the Australian Tax Office, I had our accountant fully investigate the tax situation and what that meant for my own finances. I knew it would be too late to change anything after we implemented a strategy. I sought advice and a legal opinion regarding the restructuring, and it was approved. I even had a verbal OK from the Australian Tax Office.

Presented with the evidence and advice supporting my decision, I forged ahead. Five years later, I got a letter from the tax department informing me I owed approximately six million dollars in back taxes. Apparently, our Prime

Minister changed some of the tax deduction laws and made them retroactive for the previous five years.

This news was heartbreaking. But in line with my philosophies in this book, I paid it out. A few anomalies remain, and once those are sorted out, the ordeal will be finished. I have moved on, although I haven't recovered yet from the trauma it caused.

The point I'm making is that you can plan all you want, but you can't predict every possible contingency. Your preparations must allow for the unexpected cyclone that comes out of the blue and wipes out your crop. Luckily I had planned for such disaster and was able to survive. Will you be able to survive your financial crisis?

Your answer has to be yes. Set that process in motion now, so that you too will have the means at your disposal to survive. Besides, should such a disaster never befall you or your company, you will be left with even more of the spoils of your success to share with the ones you love.

Anticipate Unethical People

If life was fair, we would all be given the chance to get ahead. But life is not fair. There will always be someone waiting to take advantage of you under the presumption that "it's my right."

As a nation, we've come a long way towards helping those who are less fortunate. But we've picked up a lot of bastards in the process who take advantage of the good we have done.

I've heard it said many times: the more you do for people, the less they give in return. And the more you do for someone, the more he or she takes. I believe this only holds true for a minority of people—and thank heaven for that! The majority are considerate and well-meaning, unless cornered and under pressure.

I'm going to provide you with a strategy for dealing with unethical individuals, businesspeople, conglomerates, or even worse, bodies of government (who sometimes take action against those whose only crime is ignorance in the workings of business).

If you make a claim against someone, you'll increase your chance of winning if it costs them heartache, hardship, or money. The other way people in business can take you to the cleaners is by abruptly changing the rules. They will set targets, but bury cloaked clauses inside their agreements.

This allows them to change or move the conditions when they feel threatened. Beware, for instance, of what I call the "golden parachute" clause. This clause favours the supplier or individual and provides a way for him or her to back out of the contract.

Let me give you a concrete example. We had built a business that was dependent on our suppliers providing the product. We earned commissions on the products we sold on their behalf.

For our purposes here, we'll call the company "Beaver."

We had worked for Beaver for six months, and we had built up a bonus of $250,000 that was now due. Beaver knew they owed us that amount but informed us it wasn't due. What could we do? Sue, scream, complain, or simply accept it.

The cost and time involved in pursuing this was too great, and we were overwhelmed by the case they prepared. I had to let it go, but I made a decision that day to never deal with unethical businesspeople again. You find information about people by asking and researching.

Another example I'll cite regards an individual. We closed a division and displaced six staff members, one of whom filed an application for discrimination. She claimed the real reason we sacked her was because she was pregnant.

Once again, despite our innocence, it made no sense to defend the case. In terms of the cost or the time it would require, it was better to pay up and put a quick end to it.

In both situations, the individuals involved were unethical, dishonest, and undertook criminal action to gain a quick buck at our expense. So beware. Make sure you cross your t's and dot your i's, because people, businesses, and institutions are anxious to steal everything they can get from you.

Meet "Mr. Nice Guy"

Are you a casualty of your parents? This thought should scare you to death! Are you the type of person who seeks approval from others in your life for the sake of acceptance?

Ask your partner for his or her view on how you stack up regarding this question, because self-assessment won't work in this case. Make sure he or she understands complete honesty is required. If it turns out you do follow such a pattern, you could be poisoning your success and business.

Here's how. We often go along with people because we don't want confrontation in our lives. This has the effect of making our associates believe us, even if we're presenting them with sugarcoated lies. We may not agree with their conclusions, or our intentions could be elsewhere. None of that matters to us, because all we focus on is the approval of others rather than the business at hand.

I call such people "Mr. Nice Guy." Subconsciously, such individuals feel they are elevated above the rest of us, because they "turn the other cheek" and are "tolerant" of the views of others. But, remember, they're not necessarily agreeing with the matter under consideration (a business strategy, for example). It's simply easier to go with the flow. And, of course, they may end up doing what they want once all backs are turned.

TIP: It is a big mistake to believe you have the loyalty or trust of Mr. Nice Guy.

They are snakes in the grass. When bush walking, you make noises to try to scare snakes away. But snakes will still turn and bite when you least expect it. Ignore this warning at your peril.

The most unethical Mr. Nice type of person who has ever crossed my path was AJ. I allowed him into my business, and he took me for as much as he could until I had had enough. I stood by his side against my business partner and wife on many occasions. After paying off all his debts twice and giving him a high profile position and remuneration to match, he turned on me in my time of need.

My company had a time when it was growing too fast for its own good. We had a cash flow crisis, and I asked the directors to take a pay cut and stand down from taking holidays until the business could afford it. AJ's holidays were due, and even though he agreed up front to accept the arrangement, he secretly went out of his way to take as much as he could get. Even though I negotiated a package for him for the short-term, he made a legal partition to wind up the business and would not remove it unless I paid for all of his holidays and back pay.

Once that was settled, we didn't have the same relationship that we had built up over the previous ten years. We called it quits. AJ wasn't through with me yet, though! He strategically went out of his way to head hunt my salespeople and tried to steal our business customers to a new entity that he had set up in opposition to us.

It is people like this that have no loyalty to others. They can't be trusted to have any natural affection towards their own family let alone business partners, because they will turn on either of them when the opportunity arises.

Trusting Those Close to You

"MF" was another employee who worked for me. His story is heartbreaking and teaches a great lesson to anyone who is too trusting.

He was destitute and on his last legs financially. I trained him personally, as I had done with AJ. He was a well-accepted person, and everyone liked him because he was just so nice. Nothing was too much trouble for him. He said yes to any tasks that I asked him to do. He went out of his way to get to know all my professional contacts along with the usual introductions.

He met and built relationships with all of my key people in Australia. It wasn't until I found our sales had fallen from seven thousand a month to about one thousand that I became suspicious. I believe when you have a problem and don't know where to look, simply look at the nicest person that has influence in the area of concern.

Sure enough, it was MF. He had strategically set out to steal as much as he could from me and my business. When I confronted him about the ordeal, it was the same response that all Mr. Nice Guys give. He gave me a hangdog look and all the excuses in the book. Each excuse sounded the same. He didn't want to do it, but he had no choice. Or he didn't know why he did it, but he was sorry.

Yet when he saw the opportunity, he repaid me by continuing to steal my people, intellectual property, and as much other information as he could grab. Until I took legal action, that is. It's heartbreaking for me to come across this type of individual, because it makes one question human nature. It makes it all the harder to trust the next person.

THE ALTERNATIVE

Conversely, I want to introduce another person who was heavily involved in my business. I'll call him "MK." This person was only about twenty-years-old and straight from university. I gave him his first job. MK took the same road as AJ but with different ethics.

Everything was too much for him. While he excelled at the tasks I gave him, he wasn't happy and told me so. In the beginning, I gave him the worst jobs I could find to see if he had perseverance and gumption. He came to me for advice from time to time, and to my surprise, he took it and applied it to his situation.

From a telemarketer to account executive, he moved up learning the business the hard way. He studied, and he used trial and error. He stuck through the good and bad times on very average pay. He threatened to leave many times. On one occasion, he did so for a short while. Then he came to his senses and came back to work for me again.

He always had an opinion of how we should approach something, and we had many arguments discussing the pros and cons of his ideas. Generally the outcome was good. He progressed to office manager and then to operations manager. Eventually he became a 50 percent partner in the business. This individual has been the light of my business career. He has demonstrated the qualities of loyalty and dependability. But most of all, his word is his bond.

It warms my heart to have him work with me and restores my confidence in human nature. He has become a close friend and business partner, and we have a friendship that will last for many years to come.

REMEMBER: Beware where you place your trust. Even a sleeping snake can bite you twice.

Let me tell you the story about the frozen snake. A mountaineer was halfway up the face of a mountain when he noticed a beautifully coloured snake encased about three inches beneath the surface of the ice.

He had heard that if an animal was frozen quickly enough while it was hibernating, it could be brought back to life so long as the thawing process was slow and carefully administered.

The man took the snake and placed it carefully in front of his cabin fire for nearly three weeks. Finally, as if by magic, he saw movement as the snake began to wake. Eventually the snake moved about, becoming familiar with its surroundings. Then, as the mountaineer stooped down to offer it some food, the snake suddenly lunged at the man, biting him on the hand.

The man was shocked. Why would this snake bite him after all he had done for it? To his surprise the snake reared up and said, "It's in my nature to bite. You should have known that."

The man promptly grabbed his hatchet and cut off the snake's head. The moral of this story is to remember that someone you help may not value what you do. If it's in their nature, they are quite capable of biting the hand that feeds them without even blinking an eye.

Unscrupulous Business Associates

The other area to be wary of is your external business relationships. You leave yourself vulnerable to attack by unethical people like these by being ethical yourself. Let me illustrate what I mean.

If you promote your business as an opportunity that requires hard work in order to gain the rewards, you are at a disadvantage. Others who don't have your scruples have no problem promising riches for little effort. People want instant gratification, so many will be tempted to take the easy way out.

The only way to counteract that is to be candid with your people. Tell them the truth. Warn them about the wolves that will take advantage of their insecurities and trusting nature. Understand, however, that your warning will fall on some deaf ears.

 ## *The Best Decisions I Made*

PREPARE YOURSELF FOR OPPORTUNITY

The way to become the best you can is through self-development. Learning is the greatest gift. It is the doorway to knowledge, and as you know, knowledge is the nucleus of power. Learning allows you to recognize when opportunity knocks on the door.

Educating yourself in the field of your choice will make you an expert. Experts can demand the highest incomes in the world. Being an expert grants you the respect of your peers, and others will not be able to legitimately knock your efforts.

Never Burn Bridges

The people you already know can often help you get ahead either now or in the future. It's easy to wind down a good relationship just because a person has upset you. Every day, people end friendships and relationships because they have offended each other.

I am amazed people take such a short-term view of life. Often, the way forward is not to burn your bridges of friendship but to simply adjust the depth of closeness rather than discarding the relationship entirely.

Never say to someone in the heat of the moment that you are finished with them. Choose a smart way to finish with them if you want, but don't say that's what you are doing. You never know when you may need them in the future. Never burn your bridges. Keep them passable.

 Action Plan and Tasks

Project Management
My Thermometer Symbol

I introduced this tool at a sales seminar to demonstrate how to monitor successful sales. My wife drew it on a piece of cardboard, and I had it mounted on one of the walls of the sales training room.

The primary reasons I hung it there were:

- It visually displayed our sales progress.

- It served as a reminder of my obligation to their success.

- It allowed prospective salespeople and dealers to easily grasp how well they could do if they applied the same rules and techniques in their own businesses.

- It influenced the trainees to join our organization when they completed their training.

If you would like to see a picture of what the thermometer looked like, go to: http://wugrav.wustl.edu/people/CMW/thermometer.jpg.

I drew indicator lines between the dollar amounts affixed to the thermometer, and I recorded our results on that line as we achieved them.

This provided us with a running total of the actual volume of sales we had at any given moment. The amount of business never went down. It was added to the previous figure because our customers were billed every month that they chose to stay with us.

In other words, every month we would send them a bill for the phone calls they made the previous month. That was how the Rule of 78 worked.

The Yearly Planner

The yearly planner proved an invaluable tool for managing an entire year's activity throughout Australia. For each city, I selected training dates and blocked out the allocated time along with the rest of the following week's activity, such research, home duties, and attending set appointments.

Whenever I was at a particular location, I would also teach:

- Recruiting

- Interviewing

- Selling techniques

- Motivation techniques

- Problem solving

- Self-improvement

All of these training programs were available on tape, so dealers who didn't have access to the face-to-face training could access the same information. Every activity was added to this yearly planner to prevent double bookings. It also allocated blocks of time for relaxation.

MASTER STRATEGY 5

TRAITS OF CHARISMA

CHAPTER 6 ›› In this chapter you'll learn how to turn your individual strengths into an ironclad fortress against failure. You will do this by:

- Applying the principles I'll outline

- Identifying your specific weaknesses to work on

- Passing on what you've learned to others

TIP: You can only do what you can do—and all you can do is good enough!

In order to begin these tasks, you need to understand the foundations of effort and that special quality of personal magnetism that allows one to influence others. I'm talking, of course, about charisma.

A Lion's Share of Pressure

A lion guards its kill covetously. If you understand why, it will help propel you ahead quickly in your business. In order to understand this better, I'm going to tell you my interpretation of a story from a movie called *The Ghost and the Darkness*.

The movie was about aggressive man-eating lions in the Kenyan region of Tsavo and a British engineer named Colonel John H. Patterson. This is the true story of Colonel Patterson's formidable task of building a railway bridge across the Tsavo River in 1900.

Naturally, there were scores of workers engaged in various tasks on this bridge. The lions lived in this area, and on a regular basis, they attacked and killed an astounding number of the workers. In the course of only a few weeks, two of the lions were responsible for over one hundred deaths!

Colonel Patterson was a marksman and a renowned hunter. But his attempts to hunt down the lions and halt the bloodshed met with no success. So Patterson hired another famous hunter. This man brought with him people from the Masai tribe who were famous for their bravery and lion-tracking skills. They also failed.

The Trap

The colonel's next scheme was to build what looked like a cabin but was actually a trap. The lions would be lured into the cabin, where, unbeknownst to them, marksmen would be waiting. The marksmen knew the lions would be within six feet of them, but they also knew they would be protected by a barrier of thick steel bars.

The marksmen were confident about the plan as well as their ability to shoot the lions dead at the close range. They waited all of the first night and through the second night. Nothing happened. By the third night, they were quite tired and eventually drifted off to sleep.

Naturally, one of the lions picked this moment to enter the trap. The door behind the lion clanged shut, setting off the lion's ferocious roar. The tribesmen awoke. They were confused and terrified with only steel bars and a few feet of airspace between themselves and the angry lion.

The lion tried to rush at them, sending the tribesmen into even more of a panic. Even though the metal bars protected the shooters from being harmed, they froze from their fear, panic, and the enormous stress. They froze so badly, they couldn't even get themselves to shoot and kill the lion!

Mind Tricks

Even though the lion was only six feet away, their minds played tricks on them. Their thoughts and focus were diverted to their fear and panic rather than the task of shooting accurately. It sapped their strength and self-assurance. What had been a lion trap had been transformed by their minds into their own trap.

Eventually they tried to shoot, and bullets flew everywhere. Yet these skilled marksmen, heralded for their skill and bravery, couldn't hit an enormous lion only six feet away!

As the lion charged and lunged at the bars, they were so fearful that they actually tried to cut a hole in the back of the cabin wall in hopes of escaping. Remember, they were in no real danger. Eventually the lion was able to shove its way out of the door and make its escape.

So why couldn't they shoot this lion? They had the skill, the confidence in their abilities, and a great, effective plan.

Well, can you imagine being only six feet away from a hungry, angry lion? I'm sure you were able to quite vividly picture it while you read my account of the story! Would you agree you would be under an enormous amount of pressure whether or not you were skilled with a rifle?

There's a valuable lesson here: the wrong kind of stress and pressure will divert your focus away from the task at hand. It makes no sense to willingly put yourself under the wrong kind of pressure. Many businesspeople have been financially hurt because they never understood this simple principle.

The Wrong Kind of Stress

Pressuring yourself to write sales is a perfect example of the wrong kind of stress.

TIP: Complete the presentation (the task at hand) and the sales process.

You don't have a gun to their head, so you'll never have control over what another person wants. Complete the presentation. That is all you can control.

If you allow your focus to drift, or if you worry about the end result, you won't have your complete attention on your presentation. At that moment, nothing else in the world should be getting your attention. By the time you've completed your presentation, your prospect should have every question answered and every possible detail necessary to make an informed decision.

TIP: Never try too hard to make the sale. Measure your success on how many quality presentations you've completed.

Always complete the presentation. If you do, you can never fail. Don't say, "I haven't made a sale" because that is not how you measure your success in the learning process.

Measure success on how many presentations you've completed. All your job requires is to stay in front of a client long enough to complete the presentation. This is where your true skill can shine. And don't forget what you learned earlier. As long as you complete "x" number of presentations, you will make "y" number of sales.

The More Presentations, The Higher Your Income

Your new goal is to count completed presentations rather than the number of sales. If you don't write the sale but have completed the presentation, you still have been successful.

You can tell the difference between success and failure or a good day versus a bad day by the number of completed presentations. Don't put yourself under the pressure of having to make sales to earn an income. You will become like the lion shooters—full of fear and failure.

All the one-on-one or face-to-face interviews will put you under enough pressure as it is. But this time we're talking about the correct kind of pressure. This is the kind of pressure that motivates. You can't go through life without it. This kind of pressure forces you to grow, and when you grow in yourself, your money will grow as well.

"Good" Pressure Propels You

Why were steam-driven trains and locomotives so strong and powerful? The answer is pressure. Their boilers created it, and it was applied directly to the wheels. Increase the pressure in the boilers, and the locomotive goes faster and becomes more powerful.

Similarly, tonnes of pressurized coal become diamonds over time. Without pressure, they have little value.

Sometimes we need a mind shift to understand how the pressure that drives us is good rather than bad. Just remember that it has to be the right kind. Reject the type of pressure that causes you to fail.

When you wake up in the morning, ask yourself, "How much pressure can I be under today? What other problems and challenges can I solve today to make me a better individual?"

TIP: The more pressure you are under, the more pressure you will feel comfortable handling the next time.

The more correct pressure you find yourself facing, the more you will grow. Think of it as a crucial element in your personal growth program.

If you have a problem and you solve it, your ability to handle problems has increased. Think of a rubber band. If you stretch it enough times, it no longer returns to its original shape. Pulling the ends half an inch in opposite directions may have caused it stress before, but now it is used to stretching that far. It handles the pressure with little stress.

Now think back to when you first learned to tie your shoelaces. That's a lot of pressure for a young child. But once you had confronted and vanquished that challenge enough times, the feeling of pressure went away. Even if it still took you a long time to complete the task, you did so calmly. You were confident in your ability to see it through with success.

There is one thing to bear in mind. You can't always change or control a situation where you are under pressure. Such situations are outside your control. In these cases, try to convert it to activity. For example, if your problem is not getting enough sales, convert that to what type of activity you have to carry out to achieve the sales result desired and make the situation work for you. You will be far better off for it.

Welcome Pressure into Your Life

TIP: When you are addressing a group of people, you may feel butterflies in your stomach. Don't wish them away—welcome them.

Neither the butterflies nor the fear that accompanies them will harm you. In fact, they'll actually make you stronger.

Events that put you outside your comfort zone make you grow, and they make you feel alive, too. They needn't be traumatic. What I'm referring to are the kinds of challenges and experiences that seem fearsome at first but fill you with vitality as you rise to the occasion and overcome them. After all, if you don't grow, you will become stagnant. And you know what happens to stagnant water.

TIP: Every presentation you do increases your strength, conviction, and success rate.

Most people put themselves under pressure to be on time for appointments. While being late is discourteous, it's a tiny infraction in the larger scheme of things. It makes no sense to experience such a meaningless pressure.

If you do find yourself arriving late for a meeting or an appointment, use the experience to test your coping ability. Use it as an opportunity for personal growth.

Build Rapport

When you arrive at a meeting late, others may be a little irritated with you. They may even be downright angry! Use their mood or temperament to strengthen the bond, break the ice, and build rapport. You may say something like, "Mr. Jones, I know that you're probably a little upset with me, and I realize I'm late. In fact, you may even yell at me. I can understand that and wouldn't blame you a single bit. I'm sure that sometime in your life you've been late, and it was unavoidable. I've had one of those days today. I'm asking, please, could we put it to the side?"

What will that individual say? What could they possibly say? You've asked them for help, and only a person who's not worth dealing with wouldn't accept an apology like that.

If someone is angry, say you are sorry, ask his or her forgiveness, and make up. People respect others who don't shrink from taking responsibility. When you kiss and make up within your family, for instance, the bond is typically strengthened. Similarly, this will build rapport with the individual and help you relax so you can make your presentation.

Respect the Lions

Always remember: you are no better or worse than the customer. So don't put on airs and graces. Most of us have the same number of fingers on our hands and toes on our feet. The same blood courses through our veins. If you act too slick and savvy, you'll come off as someone who is either hiding something or has delusions of grandeur. Neither are attractive traits! Just be you.

TIP: When you know too much, people may start to doubt what you are saying.

Don't praise yourself because you believe you know everything. When somebody has a concern or they ask a question, answer without acting pompous. After all, it's likely there are things they could teach you, too.

"Try On" the Other Person's Shoes

If you learn to provide prospects and customers with what they need, they'll give you what you want. It takes an ability to listen to them, not assume what they're trying to say beforehand, and view their concerns through their eyes. Avoid jargon and communicate with them at a level that is understandable.

Be mindful of the way you answer questions. If you answer them too quickly, the customer may think you haven't thought about it, or you may come across as a know-it-all.

Take your time to answer, and you will stand out as a rare salesperson with empathy and concern for others. We've all been frustrated when others don't take the time to truly hear our concerns. Equally as frustrating is when they assume they already know what we are asking, so they don't truly "hear" us. Unfortunately, this is the norm. Treat your customers or prospects differently, and they will never forget you.

TIP: Do not answer a question straight away but always demand an answer for your own questions immediately.

That may take a while to learn, but the acquisition of that skill will put you years ahead in business. Learn these skills as part of your apprenticeship.

Become a Master

How long does it take to learn a skill like playing a guitar proficiently? I've read on average, about a thousand hours of continuous, effective learning and practice will normally produce a reasonably proficient guitar player (or other, similar skill).

Now contrast that with my experience. The time it takes to master the skills of being successful in sales may only be 120 or 130 consistent hours over a three-month period! In other words, don't give up, because this is very attainable. It does take persistence, though, so it is important to make this practice a part of your daily life.

TIP: You have to master rebuttals to objections, questions, or concerns.

Never give an answer straight away without fully analysing what the customer or prospect wants to know. Take a moment to view it from their perspective. I like to count to five before I answer a question, even if I know the answer. This allows a moment to fully consider the other person and make sure I haven't misinterpreted the question.

A Statement or Question's Real Meaning

Just because someone says, "I don't like your product," that may not mean what it sounds like. For instance, a person who truly doesn't like your product may say this, but so might someone who doesn't understand it and consequently sees no value in it.

In this example, if you don't ask questions to discern what they're really thinking, it's likely that you will launch into a response that makes no sense to them.

TIP: talk to them as though you are talking to your mother, father, or someone close to you.

When a customer asks you a question or a potential customer expresses a concern, treat that concern or question as very important and answer it from a gut level. The person who asked the question has cause for concern. Alleviate that concern.

Consider the **Feel, Felt, Found** approach. This is a technique that builds empathy and identifies you with the individual.

Here's an example of Feel, Felt, Found in action:

"Look, I **feel** the same way, Mrs. Jones. I **felt** that way at one stage when I first heard about it, but I **found** if I did this, it worked well."

Note how I'm talking to the imaginary Mrs. Jones at a gut level. Also, it addresses the specifics of her concern, so it doesn't come off as scripted. Remember, everyone in business is much more used to dealing with people who appear to be saying the same things that they have a thousand times before.

Talk to people at the gut level, and it will make an impact on them.

Communication Skills

The people you are talking to are not stupid. But lack of communication can make people appear this way, so don't misinterpret this. Good communication requires practice and patience, and they may not have devoted the same attention to it as you.

These people want help from you, and they look up to you. You are the source of information and inspiration. Make sure you give it to them in a manner that can truly be useful to them.

TIP: When you deliver a visual presentation, lay it out slowly and deliberately. Treat it reverently.

Be gentle with your materials, show it has value, and people will respect what you say.

TIP: Before you start, ensure the person has an open mind.

Unblock the person's mind before you begin your presentation. No matter what you say and how good your delivery, it will all be for naught if the person's mind is closed.

They may recognize the importance of what you offer and want to listen in theory, but unless you grab and maintain their interest, their attention will drift. They may have already established an opinion of what you will say and have let their mind focus on other business matters. If this is the case, their mind is blocked.

Compelling Force of the Eyes

You've heard it said before: always look someone in the eye. But have you ever been told why?

When you look into a person's eyes, you may be able to read if there is an unsaid problem, a concern arising, or if the person is lying to you.

The eyes are the windows to the soul, heart, and mind. Look at the pupils. If they shrink in diameter while they are talking to you, it may indicate that they dislike you, or they are not being honest. On the other hand, if the pupil dilates, there is a good chance they are responding favourably to you and are being truthful.

TIP: When you look into someone's eyes, take note of the colour.

Don't stare, of course. You don't want to make them uncomfortable.

But take a moment and observe the colour of their eyes. Why? It concentrates your attention upon them, quiets your mind, and reorients your focus.

It also builds rapport. A chemical reaction occurs between two people when they look each other in the eyes. It's a sudden bridge between two minds, and it allows each to observe subtle nonverbal cues. This, of course, brings up the other primary reason for looking into someone's eyes when you've asked them to buy something from you.

The Eyes Betray Dishonesty

Say you've asked your prospect if they're going to buy from you. It's easier for them to give a dishonest answer if you're not looking them in the eye. On the other hand, if you wait until you're one-on-one with them, you have their full attention, and you're looking right into their eyes, you're more likely to get an honest response.

That honest answer will provide you with clues how to proceed. Perhaps you need to determine their objections or concerns? Maybe it's time to move on to the next prospect. In either case, without the insight provided by looking them in the eye, you wouldn't have had a chance figuring out the correct course of action.

TIP: Enthusiasm translates to believability.

Mistrust is a normal part of doing business. The antidote to mistrust is communication and believability.

If you want someone to believe what you are saying, you have to look them in the eye and say it enthusiastically. Your voice should express lively exuberance in the pitch (tone), pace (speed), and power (volume).

How deeply do you believe in your product? The last four letters of "enthusiasm" is IASM, which stands for "I Am Sold Myself." Learn about the product you are selling, and become a supportive, enthusiastic voice for it.

Know and Use What You Are Selling

You have to be familiar with the advantages of your merchandise, products, and/or services. You have to know how it compares with the competition. The best way to do this is to become an avid user of the product or service.

By becoming a regular customer yourself, you'll be better equipped to consider what you're selling from the point of view of your prospects. Pay particular attention to the customer benefits your product/service offers. What can it do for them, and how can it change their lives for the better?

TIP: Speak in terms of benefits rather than features.

Many salespeople make the mistake of focusing too much attention on the features of their product or service. These usually mean little to a prospect, and it's a good way to lose his or her attention. For instance, if you recite specs to the prospect, his or her eyes are likely to glaze over. But if you tell them instead that the "such and such feature will cut their production time in half," you'll grab their full attention.

TIP: Check back with customers to make sure they're making a profit from what you sold them.

Build your fortress

Financial flexibility results from building a very large organization. Your company will keep expanding through the diligence, effort, and expertise of yourself as well as those you hire.

Imagine you have ten, fifteen, or one hundred people doing what you are doing in your business.

TIP: Increase profitability by increasing the number of people in your organization.

Active Listening

Pay close, rapt attention to what prospects and customers have to say. Our expectations and inner dialogue can drown out what we need to hear. By developing your ability to actively listen, you'll be better able to satisfy the needs of your prospects and customers. And they will reward you handsomely for this.

Develop their need into a strong desire. Remember, if you give them what they want, they will give you what you want.

The Post-Sale Follow-Through

If your company offers a thirty day 100 percent money-back guarantee, use that to its fullest advantage. It is a powerful way to build rapport, and that translates into future sales or references.

We never forget businesspeople that treat us fairly and fulfill their obligations. With that in mind, always accept a customer's return cheerfully, and process it quickly. Bear in mind that such moments are often awkward for the customer, and they'll be grateful for any effort on your part to alleviate that stress. You may have lost one sale, but you may have gained a customer for life.

Do take a moment, though, to ask why your customer has cancelled. The insight may prove valuable further down the line. Use the Feel, Felt, and Found technique you learned earlier in this chapter. Remember, you're not trying to change the customer's mind. This is strictly an information and learning experience.

As stated earlier, make sure you check back with your customers to make sure they're making a profit from your product or service. Rapport needs to be tended. And don't forget to ask your customers for referrals. They are a normal part of doing business and invaluable during the early years of your company.

TIP: Customer loyalty lasts longer if contact is maintained on a regular basis.

Step-By-Step Agreements

Socrates, the Greek philosopher and teacher, used a technique of persuasion that may prove helpful to you. I won't go too deeply into the Socratic Method here. But in a nutshell, the goal is to persuade a listener of a larger point by leading them down a discussion path and getting them to agree to a series of related but smaller points along the way. The idea is that the smaller agreements would eventually persuade the listener of the validity in Socrates' original point.

These smaller agreements are similar to a sales technique called "tie downs." It's a way of "educating" a prospect about how your product/service will benefit them by breaking down your pitch into its component parts, each of which is not easily disputed. It's extremely effective, but I like to use it sparingly. If used to excess, this method can actually annoy prospects.

Some basic tie down statements that you'll find useful are:

- Aren't they?

- Doesn't it?

- Don't you agree?

- Isn't that right?

- Isn't that true?

Asking the Right Questions

There are hundred of other tie downs that can be placed at the ends of a sentence to persuade prospects to say yes.

TIP: Selling is the art of asking the right questions to gain each incremental yes that eventually leads your prospect to the final major yes.

The key is to learn how to use these in a way that sounds natural and not manipulative. Try practicing putting the tie down at the beginning of a sentence.

Practice the examples below by listening to how they sound aloud. Sometimes changing a word or two helps the sentence flow more naturally. The first example is:

"Many companies are tired of excessive costs today, aren't they?"

Now try changing it up by moving the tie down to the beginning of the sentence: "Aren't a lot of companies tired of excessive costs today?"

Tie Down Forms

1. Standard Form: "Once you get the discounts, you can really control the bill, can't you?"

2. Inverted Form (the tie down comes first): "You can really control the bill once you get the discounts..."

3. Internal Form (the tie down is in the middle.) "Once you get the discounts, you can really control the bill well."

Simple techniques like these are easy to implement and cost you nothing. But they can dramatically increase your success rate and earning power.

A good way to research this method is to simply turn your radio to the news or some form of talk radio. Notice tie downs are constantly being used. Make mental notes of which ones are effective. Practice your tie downs out loud. Don't overlook the splendid opportunity to sharpen your techniques every time you buy or sell something.

The Two-Headed Tie Down

An alternative to the classic tie down is to ask a question for which you provide two different answer options. This is particularly useful, for example, when you're trying to nail down an appointment in order to give your sales presentation.

Consider, for instance, if you ask your prospect: "Should I come by this afternoon?" What answer would most buyers give you? You can bet you'd lose a high percentage to the answer no.

Instead, offer your prospect two time options. For example: "Mr. Turner, I'll be in your area this afternoon. Which would be more convenient for me to stop by—around 2:00, or would you prefer 3:00?"

You stand a much higher chance that your prospect will either pick one of the offered choices or will come back with another alternative time choice. Either way, you've gotten what you sought—an appointment time.

I was very fortunate when I entered the sales business. I had a teacher who insisted that I learn the ropes thoroughly, so I could avoid some of the hardships and heartache that dog you when you're inexperienced. That didn't mean I never had setbacks. Rather, I knew how to emotionally and logistically handle those setbacks as they arose.

Others who don't learn these lessons fail quickly. I know from firsthand experience! There were times I was negative, depressed, and ready to give up on selling. I had to call upon and apply what I had learned or be forced to give up my dreams and take a job with an income ceiling.

TIP: Maintain control of a meeting by answering a prospect's question.

This allows you to lead them into the next step of your selling sequence.

No matter what it is you're selling, you will probably be asked questions that can be answered with a yes or no. You will constantly be asked by people to give them information, but if you answer them immediately, you will get nothing from them in return.

TIP: Listen. Then listen more. Ask questions, but above all else, listen.

Your prospect will be impressed by your attentiveness.

Professional salespeople use two types of questions.

1. Discovery questions

2. Leading questions

Discovery questions reveal what your prospect's needs are as they relate to your product or service. Your probing questions uncover hints about what your prospect is looking for, and this gives you the opportunity to offer your product/service as solutions for these needs.

Leading questions are phrased in a way that suggests a specific answer. In other words, you lead the prospect through your questions so that they'll state your selling point for you.

Discovery questions are not effective if you're not fully focused on your task of unearthing information. You can't be on "autopilot."

AN EXAMPLE

Somebody says to you as you walk into a store, "May I help you?"

The standard answer is, "I'm just looking." Countless retail salespeople ask this very same question every single day, and they get variations of the same answer.

It never seems to occur to them to stop asking this generic "non-question." And they never seem to realize that their question means nothing to the customer. The customers' response is given as automatically as the question was asked.

The day a clerk decides to stop greeting customers this way—the day he or she finally goes off autopilot—is the day he or she qualifies for a more advanced selling position.

Here's a better way to welcome customers: "Good morning. If you are looking for our super bargains, they're on the left side of the store. If you have any questions, just let me know. In the meantime, please feel free to look around."

Because that salesperson has already gotten a foot in the door, he or she can come back later to the customer and ask, "I was wondering how you are doing?" And continue on from there.

TIP: A "say no" question is any question that can be answered with a yes or no. If you only present that option, you stack the odds against yourself.

My experience is people will pick no rather than yes more than 50 percent of the time when a salesperson gives them those choices. Therefore, the first rule of discovery questioning is to never ask a "say no" question.

It's All About Persuasion

Think about it. When you're trying to persuade someone, you're dealing with positives—how a product or service will benefit your prospect; how cost-effective it will be; how it will improve productivity or profits. Salespeople who are guided by this concept understand that they can't be sidetracked by side issues. In other words, making their prospect think of any negativity will not help them get the sale. It will likely prevent it.

As a general rule, it's better to ask rather than tell, and it's better for your interaction with your prospect to be conversational.

Ask the discovery questions that will reveal how best your product or service can benefit them. Then ask questions that lead them to the conclusion that your product/service takes care of their needs.

The three principles to keep in mind here are:

1. Establish a bond or rapport before you go for control of the discussion. How much time this will require varies. But keep this point in mind: you'll stack the odds against yourself if you insist on trying to lead every prospect.

2. Give people a moment to think and process. Their immediate response to the idea of spending money is likely to be negative, so give that immediate response time to fade and the logic of your presentation to sink in. For the same reasons, always pause before directly answering their questions.

3. Once someone has indicated they are happy with your answers and presentation, use a closing sequence of questions to secure the sale immediately. More on this later.

Trust

Building trust and selling your expertise is a skill.

TIP: To be persuasive, we must be believable. And to be believable, we must be truthful.

When a salesperson betrays a lack of integrity, it taints the validity of everything he or she says. The prospect or customer is likely to distrust everything that comes out of that salesperson's mouth. It's only human.

TIP: One way a salesperson may appear trustworthy is by taking action that is against his or her self-interest.

If we're convinced that a salesperson has little to gain and perhaps something to lose, we won't distrust his or her credibility when trying to persuade us to buy.

For example, let's say a convicted heroin smuggler delivers a speech that states that the criminal justice system is unfair, and criminals are the victims of an unjust social system. Would his comments influence you? Probably not. Most people would assume his points were biased and, therefore, have little validity.

Now imagine if that same individual argued instead that the criminal system was too soft on crime. What if he said sentences were too short, and prisoners should do hard labour whilst inside?

Would his comments influence you? Certainly. One of the most effective ways to win acceptance in people's minds is to first admit a negative, and then turn it around into a positive.

Candour Is Very Disarming

Candour must be managed with great skill. First of all, the negative you admit to must be widely perceived as a negative. It has to trigger instant agreement in your prospect's mind. Then you have to shift gears quickly to the positive.

TIP: The purpose of candour isn't to apologize. The purpose of candour is to convince your prospect that what you say is the truth.

On the other hand, the easiest way to destroy your credibility is to oversell or exaggerate. The daily bombardment of sales pitches and political hype has made everyone very sceptical of individuals who seem too enthusiastic, or "salesy."

TIP: One of the best ways to increase your credibility is to openly admit the weaknesses or disadvantages associated with your proposal.

It is a deceptively disarming technique. The best salespeople increase their credibility by pointing out the disadvantages or the risks associated with their product. Your truthfulness will score points, but it will also demonstrate your ultimate confidence in what you sell.

In order to be credible, the following three conditions must be met:

THE FIRST LEVEL

You have to build your **personal** credibility and convince your prospect of it.

THE SECOND LEVEL

You have to sell the credibility of your **ideas.** And if your propositions are controversial or fly in the face of conventional wisdom, you'll need to be armed with overwhelming evidence supported by independent research.

THE THIRD LEVEL

You have to sell the credibility of the **organization** that you represent.

Build Your Reputation on Openness and Honesty

Never oversell your position with exaggerated claims. Exaggeration weakens the rest of your case, even in areas where you're being truthful. In fact, if you think your audience will not believe a truthful claim you make, it may be smarter to avoid making it at all.

FOR EXAMPLE:

Let's say you're presenting the discounts of your product to a board of directors. Let's assume your product is a utility service and the savings to them is $10,000 a month. If you don't think they will believe they can save that much, I suggest you lower the dollar amount to a more credible level.

TIP: Never claim more than you think your audience will believe.

Your product or service may be the best, but if you can't convince people of it, you're better off moderating your claims. A common error is the assumption that others will trust you from the moment you start speaking. This is a big mistake, especially if you haven't first taken the time to build rapport.

Take every opportunity to show that your word is your bond, even after you've built up credibility. This will keep suspicion at bay.

Make a Good First Impression

What kind of first impression do you make? If you don't make the grade within the first handful of minutes, you've probably already lost the sale.

When we meet someone for the first time, we look at them in this way:

First, we scan the face and eyes; **second**, we look at the body; **third** we examine clothing; **fourth**, we listen to the tone of voice; **fifth**, if appropriate, we shake hands and see how that feels; **sixth**, we listen to the person's words.

Research shows it takes just two minutes to make your first impression, and within four minutes, our initial impressions are established. It can take as many as six to eight meetings to overcome a bad initial impression. And you might not even be given a second chance!

That isn't to say first impressions are infallible. They can mislead people. Prejudice and bias affects all people when they form their first impressions.

Biased Judgments

When we first meet people who are an abnormal size, have a disability, are unattractive, or somehow appear different than us, we often prejudge them. That's human nature.

How we dress can be read as statements of deep and personal values. That's why it's important to do your homework on the individual you are going to visit. If we want the greatest chance of making a sale, we have to take this into consideration.

We're Judged on How We Dress

Whether those who observe us are consciously aware of it or not, they judge us by the clothes we wear. If you dress neatly, people are much more likely to trust you. The right clothing choices can allow you to communicate authority, confidence, and professionalism. Uniforms, judges' wigs, and doctors' white coats are example of this. Business suits express the same thing.

The dark blue pinstripe suit communicates the greatest sense of authority. Although casual dress is weaving its way into the corporate world, such dress must be used with great caution. Many customers still associate casual dress with a casual, lax attitude.

Power Talk

Let's refer to the type of person who uses power in his or her spoken word as a power talker. A power talker speaks assertively when talking. They describe themselves and their beliefs positively and confidently. For example, instead of saying, "Well, it's only my opinion of course," or "I could be wrong," they say, "I believe."

TIP: Numerous studies show that speakers with good verbal skills come across as more credible, confident, and convincing.

On the other hand, speakers who hesitate or use language that conveys powerlessness lack credibility. They are judged as weak and ineffective. Power talkers accept responsibility and avoid the language of victimization. They speak decisively, and they are smart persuaders and straight talkers. They don't waffle.

They get straight to the point and say exactly what they mean. Decisive speakers project credibility and confidence. Someone who waffles continually over certain issues is perceived as showing a weakness in credibility and intelligence.

Power talkers also speak with integrity while avoiding phrases that make people question their sincerity and honesty. Instead of saying, "To be perfectly honest, we had to reprimand Peter for poor performance," they would say, "We had to reprimand Peter for giving bad advice."

Power talkers do not use what are referred to as intensifiers. These are modifiers that are tacked onto sentences. They are intended to intensify the meaning of the words they modify. In reality, they are meaningless and often have the exact opposite intended effect. A couple of examples are "very definitely" and "surely."

They also avoid tag questions, which are the added questions tacked onto the end of a statement:

"This plan will cost too much, don't you think?"

Tag questions produce uncertainty and make one seem less credible. Unless you truly want the listener to give you feedback, you should use tag questions sparingly.

For similar reasons, power talkers avoid disclaimers:

"I'm not an expert in this field, but . . . "

Powerless speakers use "please" and "thank you" excessively. Overdoing politeness communicates timidity and uncertainty. If you have made a mistake or inconvenienced someone, apologize and that's it. However, if you apologize for a situation over which you had no control, you're placing yourself in a submissive position. If you feel you have to comment on the situation at all, simply state the problem and detail the solution.

Selling the Sizzle

You've heard the expression, "sell the sizzle, not the steak." But what does that mean? It's very simple. The steak represents the product and the sizzle represents benefits.

Features are cold, remote, and impersonal. Benefits grab attention and speak directly to your prospect or customer. While prospects can be interested in features, it is the benefits that will seal the deal. Sell the tan, not the sun. Sell the envy, not the car.

Qualifications

Remember, you're selling yourself as well as your product or service. This is the wrong time to be humble about your qualifications and the honours, certifications, education, and awards you've earned. Be sure that you display and promote evidence of these achievements. They help communicate your credibility, skills in persuasion, and ability to follow through.

I'll go so far as to say that people who are too embarrassed and ashamed to display their certificates on their walls, or people that don't like others knowing they've earned recognition in higher education, suffer from low self-esteem.

Fear of Loss

TIP: People are motivated more by the fear of losing something than by gaining something of equal value.

Why do losses loom larger than gains in our minds? People are much more sensitive to negative than positive stimuli. Think about how good you feel today. Then try to imagine how much better you could feel. There are a few things that would make you feel better, but the number of things that would make you feel worse is unbounded.

TIP: The sales pitch that stresses potential loss is the most persuasive.

Instead of talking about the extra customers they will gain, emphasize the customers they would lose to their competitors.

Humour Grabs Attention

Humour is the most powerful of all motivation techniques in selling. Once you've got people laughing, you've got their attention, and they'll listen attentively to almost anything you tell them.

So how do you use humour to persuade? It can gain attention, create rapport, and make a message more memorable. If it is used appropriately, it also relieves tension, enhances relationships, and motivates people.

TIP: If I can get you to laugh at me, you will like me more. It will make you more open to my ideas.

By laughing at a point I make, you implicitly acknowledge that the point is true. The cardinal rule in using humour is to add the humour after you've planned your message and made a list of key points you want to make.

Your humour should introduce, summarize, or highlight one or more of your points. When you're using it to persuade, it is important to make it relevant. The mark of an unskilled persuader is that he or she uses irrelevant humour. To be effective, humour must make a point.

MASTER STRATEGY 6

STEPS TO DYNAMIC
PERSONAL DEVELOPMENT

CHAPTER 7 » What are the secrets? What does it take to bring about success in business and wealth acquisition? Does it require extensive education, experience, special skills, or know-how?

All these can help. But I believe the critical components are personal development and learning as much as possible about your specialty or interest.

If you are going to manage any kind of business, you must develop a capacity for leadership. I'm not just talking about the mechanics of leadership. I'm also referring to the people skills that draw others to follow you. And it bears repeating, this is important no matter what type of business you're in.

Why Businesses Fail

Businesses fail for two reasons. It's likely to occur if the company is undercapitalized. In other words, they do not have the financial means to pay the costs of running and developing the business.

The second reason businesses fail is if the operation's leaders lack management and people skills. It doesn't matter what other prowess you possess. If you don't have enough capital to survive the lean times or the management and leadership skills to overcome certain challenges, you've probably already lost. Without capital and leadership, you will lose money from all sides of the business.

How do you directly enhance your management skills? Do you have any? If you do possess such abilities, how did you get them? How are you going to gain them if you don't already have them?

From this chapter and the previous chapters, you are learning skills such as how to lead, how to recruit, how to train, and how to operate your business.

Learning from Those Who Went before You

You can go to university to read and memorize management techniques. But university won't teach you everything you need to know about running a successful business. You'll learn the theories and generalities, but it can't provide you the nitty-gritty, day-to-day operational experience. You also can't learn the specifics of the industry you're in or the finely honed talents of someone skilled in sales.

You need "the school of hard knocks" for that. I can tell you that with authority, because that's my alma mater. This was also true for many of my associates and employees.

You can gain a step-up in your real-world skills by reading and learning from successful businesspeople that have already gone down the path you're heading. Tapes, books, and manuals are excellent resources for gleaning from the experience of the best and brightest.

Everything you learn from this book, for instance, has either been put into practice by me or someone in my organization. How do I know? Because I started the company, and everything I have today is a result of the very strategies I've described in this book.

Whatever methods of learning you choose to use, there is something you should keep in mind:

Time doesn't stand still.

> You need to constantly learn how to grow your business. You need to build relationships with people that will someday produce fruit, and you need to develop your leadership strengths to the next level. You just can't afford to stand still.

Trust first. But don't let anyone cheat you twice.

> Do you live a life that people can readily respect? Do others speak of you as a person of honour? Are you someone whose word is trusted without question? Is your work ethic valued and emulated?

These are among the critical components of leadership. Leaders also trust and treat people equally, unless they've been given a clear reason not to.

If someone does try to do the wrong thing by you, don't let your emotion dictate your response. Take action to control and turn around the situation. Forgive everything except disloyalty and dishonesty.

TIP: If a person is not suitable for your business, discard them.

You only want ethical, hardworking people on your team.

If you find yourself with a lot of employees who don't want to do anything, lead by example. Let them see you blazing the trail by working harder than anyone else. That will rub off on them. You establish the "normal" work level at your business. Most of them will automatically adapt to meet this level.

Judge your employees on their performance and work habits. Those are the things that affect your bottom line. A given employee doesn't need to be well-educated, well-versed in the English language, or have extraordinary math skills. What matters is if they make you and your company profit.

Let me illustrate what I mean with a story I once read about a newly hired travelling salesman. The gentleman wrote his first report to the head office, and it stunned the brass in the sales department because it was obvious the new person was illiterate. This is what he wrote:

"Dear Bos,

I have seen this outfit which ain't never bot a dimes worth of nothing from us and I sole them a couple hunerd thousand dolars of gusds. Then I sole them another half a millyon.

I am now going to Chicawgo."

The sales manager faced a dilemma. On the one hand, he felt he couldn't possibly risk the embarrassment of having such an illiterate representative out in the field. But on the other hand, the salesman had nailed a difficult account and had brought a lot of dollars into the company.

Unable to make the decision, the sales manager dumped the problem in the lap of the CEO with surprising results. The following morning, the staff was amazed to see two letters posted on the bulletin board—the letter from the salesman and this memo from the CEO:

"We ben spending two much time tyring to spel instead of trying to sel. Le'ts watch thoes sales. I think everybody shud read these letters from Gooch, who is on the rode doin a grate job for us, and you shud go out and do like he done."

The Attitude of Achievers

People who achieve:

- Choose to believe the problems life offers are simply opportunities, challenges, and possibilities.

- Believe in their capabilities to tackle, cope with, and overcome life's challenges. Derive meaning, satisfaction, and happiness from defeating them.

- Are goal-directed and have the personal discipline to keep themselves on course.

- Believe in delayed gratification rather than the poison of instant gratification.

- Take responsibility for themselves, their decisions, their actions, and the consequences thereof.

- Are committed to reality.

- Are eternal optimists who always persevere until they reach their objectives.

TIP: Most people who achieve have an unshakeable belief in themselves, their own work, and their capacities.

Such people eliminate distractions and focus their attentions on the relevant task at hand.

I recall someone asking me, "Dan, what sort of qualities do you admire in people?"

I pondered his question and noticed something interesting about the respective traits he and I discussed that afternoon. In order to illustrate this, I'd like you to take just a few moments to do the exercise below.

Start by picturing someone in your mind who you greatly admire. You may see that person as a role model that you'd like to emulate. Now think of the qualities that you admire about this person.

What would those be? Maybe it's integrity. Perhaps it's how decisive they can be or their focus. Maybe it's their enthusiasm, charisma, honesty, generosity, confidence, or lack of fear. Write each of these qualities you admire in the space provided below:

_____

_____

_____

_____

_____

_____

Now look at your list. (If you haven't completed it, don't go on. Go back and complete it first.) Notice something distinctive about these qualities you've listed? Look closely. Few, perhaps even none, of what you've listed are skills. They are attitudes!

- -

TIP: The items you listed are attitudes you admire in people. Attitudes are personality traits that reflect who a person is, what they believe, and what they are made of.

- -

The deep respect we feel for individuals is generally because we value their attitude. It's rarely simply because of their skills.

Given this fact, what are the personal attributes of a leader or a winner? If we identify and learn how to emulate these traits, we can become leaders and winners too. What follows are descriptions of three such attributes that most high achievers possess: a philosophy of life; an ongoing and continuing program of self-development; and a well thought-out, structured plan for achieving goals and dreams.

A Life-Defining Philosophy

People find it easy to talk about what they don't like or what they don't want to happen, but most find it nearly impossible to talk about their philosophy of life. People generally don't look past what they are doing in the present, and that is a shame.

We can excuse a young teenager who hasn't left school yet for not knowing what he or she wants out of life. But what about adults? If we can't answer that question, we don't have a philosophy about life. And that's just not going to cut it.

TIP: A winner constantly defines his or her philosophy for success.

What Do I Mean by a "Philosophy of Life?"

Think of your philosophy as what many refer to as your "journey." It's the beliefs and the process you adopt in order to reach your goals. You gradually attain this philosophy through a process of personal development.

Many of us will stick a picture of something we greatly desire on our refrigerator or maybe on our computer monitor. Perhaps it's an awe-inspiring car. We do this, of course, as a reminder of something we're striving for and to motivate us when we falter.

This method can meet those limited needs nicely. But all you're presenting to yourself are the end results. What you don't see is how to go down the path or what you do along that path that ensures you reach your desired goal.

TIP: "Success is a journey; not the destination." Your life philosophy is the path that makes reaching your goals possible.

Bear in mind, too, that a goal doesn't define your life. Once you attain it, you move on to the next step and the next step after that. It's your philosophy of life.

Constant Self-Development Makes Leaders Succeed

I remember once being interviewed for a job. I walked into a rich, plush office. There was carpet on the walls, thick, luxurious red carpet on the floor, and an enormous carved oak desk that reeked of power and wealth. Behind the desk, along the back wall, were bookcases. Can you guess what kind of books filled these cases?

They were books about self-development.

TIP: Self-development books are tools for success.

If you don't read self-help books, you are denying yourself the benefits of personal development as well as the ability to grow and become a leader and a winner.

Think about the people you admire. Ask them if they read many self-help books. Chances are, most will report that they do currently or did at one time read these books.

How many books do you read a month? I get up around 5:00 AM each morning and dive into whatever book I'm reading at the time. I keep it on my bedside, so I won't lose track of it. I also keep another in the bathroom and one at the breakfast table.

This isn't to say that all self-development books are of value. Be careful of those written by authors who don't have any personal experience in the areas in which you are trying to develop. Such people can only teach you how to imitate a successful person. The operative word there is *imitate*. I'm sure you want more from your life than that!

What about you? Do you have a plan to help you develop as an individual? Do you have a philosophy to win?

When you get home after work, do you automatically switch on the TV? Do you spend your time wallowing in the pointless or negative? If that's the case, when are you going to have time to develop as a person? Are you content with staying stuck in your current status quo for the rest of your life?

TIP: You need to develop a system to achieve what you want in life.

If you ask someone to describe what his or her life will be like five years from now, what are the likely answers? He or she might tell you about hopes to own a house or boat or maybe go overseas on holidays. Maybe he or she hasn't really thought about that sort of thing yet.

But if you ask a successful person the same type of question, you get a completely different kind of answer. Successful people will be able to tell you what they want their life to be like, what they want to achieve, and the precise plan they've already put into play in order to achieve these goals.

TIP: Successful people know where they are headed. They have a philosophy of success, a self-development program, and a system in place to achieve their goals.

Your system has to be practical, so you can write it down and track it. It should be simple enough to be concise and easy to implement but complete enough to realistically achieve your goals.

Getting Others to Follow Your Lead

Do you remember the movie *Spartacus*? Do you remember the planning that Spartacus did to become a leader? This was his personal development. Do you remember how he did it? He trained as a slave gladiator for years.

Before he could recruit slaves and teach them to fight, he set out to learn how to do it himself. In the process, he not only learned the game inside and out, but he earned the respect of the gladiators.

One day, he was presented with an opportunity to escape. Playing on the respect he had gained, Spartacus rallied the support of the other gladiators, and together, they overcame the guards and fled.

They took off across the countryside, flush with the joy and excitement of their newly won freedom. Spartacus, however, recognized that the Romans would pursue them, and he determined that they must take the necessary steps to build an army to defend themselves.

And build an army he did—an enormously successful army that historians note as one of the largest slave armies in recorded history.

How did he accomplish this feat? Naturally, he couldn't do it on his own. He relied on followers who believed in and respected him and who were confident in placing their lives and livelihoods in his hands. The reason they respected his leadership was because his effort at personal development and the strength of his system had created a man they held in high esteem.

- -

TIP: Spartacus did more than simply have a system in place. He knew that when you believe strongly in your system, people will follow you.

- -

People will follow your leadership if you have confidence in yourself and your philosophy. It worked for Spartacus. He created an organization of incredible efficiency, and he was just one man!

A Single Leader Can Only Do So Much

Spartacus had to build up his army quickly. He realized that one leader wasn't enough to pull off such an enormous undertaking, and it was imperative that he train others to possess the same leadership qualities as himself.

Despite the urgency, he understood that he couldn't simply ask who wanted to be leaders. He also realized that he couldn't simply pick among them from those he felt had leadership qualities. How could he know if, after taking them under his wing, they wouldn't simply betray their fellow slaves to the Romans?

Here is what he did instead. Spartacus stood before the entire mass of escapees and told them that he needed people to help him defend themselves against the Romans. A number of people came out of the crowd, proclaiming their allegiance and their willingness to die for the cause.

TIP: Leaders will identify themselves through actions—not words.

This is the group from which Spartacus picked his leaders. It didn't matter if they were given towards telling others what to do or had had previous decision-making or supervising experience. Instead, he made it possible for people with the desired character traits to come to the forefront, and he was confident in his own ability to build those positive traits into strong leadership abilities.

TIP: The only way Spartacus could reach his goal was to replicate his leadership skills and responsibilities in others.

As organizations grow, the management responsibilities increase. The only way to maintain top efficiency is to delegate these increasing responsibilities to individuals who you've trained to maintain the same high level of leadership and decision-making. If you don't take that step, your business can't grow.

TIP: Once Spartacus trained his top people, they in turn trained others. Leadership abilities were spread in this way.

Develop a System

Others will flock to you and follow your example if you've developed an effective system and understand it from the ground up.

Perhaps I can best illustrate this by describing the systems I set up to enhance my telecommunications business. My systems, however, can be duplicated in many other types of industries and organizations.

Creating Your Network of Contacts

As your web of contacts increases, opportunities increase in kind. Become a networking machine, and do not let any opportunity pass by.

Be confident enough to introduce yourself to people you meet. Cement their names in your memory by using them often in conversation. Ask questions and actively listen to what they say. Remember, you sell yourself best when you talk less about yourself and allow others to freely express their needs.

Do not be discouraged by those who seem unresponsive to your advances. Nothing works 100 percent of the time, and there's another contact to be made just around the corner. Besides, you never know. You may have made a better impression than an individual initially leads you to believe. You might just be pleasantly surprised by a call someday.

Practice booking appointments until you are comfortable talking with people. Always take the lead in recruiting good quality people, and constantly keep an eye out for people who have leadership qualities. These are the ones you want to bring on board—not high position people.

TIP: Those who can put their system into play quickly and efficiently are the ones who grow their businesses into huge enterprises.

The size and clarity of your dreams will not only motivate you, but it will encourage the people around you as well. Develop a burning desire for a substantial worthwhile purpose, and it will be contagious to the leaders you cultivate.

To do this, you must identify what is important in your life. Visualize yourself as having already attained what is important. Do whatever is necessary to encourage the visualization process. Look at pictures of what you want to attain, use positive affirmations, or be around supportive people. (Supportive people can either be those that share your dreams or mentors who can help guide you towards attaining your goals.)

It is important to appreciate that business is a numbers game. You'll need to pass that understanding onto the leaders you cultivate. Teach your people how to determine the predictable patterns that allow them to determine how many no's they'll need before they can get a yes.

TIP: The quicker you go through the no's, the quicker you can find the yes's.

TIP: The one who completes the most presentations and recruits the most people to work in a business wins.

It is vitally important to be able to seize the moment by providing the correct information to a person immediately. You've got to be resourceful as a leader. You wear a number of hats.

You are the salesperson, sales manager, human resources manager, problem solver, and problem averter. In addition, you are also your own business manager. You even have your fingers in marketing, motivation, accounts, and profit.

But don't forget to harvest the crop you've sown. It rests in the expertise of the leaders you've cultivated. Don't waste this valuable resource by not asking for help if and when you need it.

A Leader Sets Up the Team Members for Success

The most important thing is to develop a dynamic team. You have to be selective when recruiting and choose only the self-motivated and tenacious.

You must have the utmost respect for your people. They pay the bills and your future wages, so give them the support they need. Set them up for success. You have to understand what they must cope with on a daily basis. I don't mean you should feel sorry for them. What I'm talking about is empathy.

TIP: Lead your team by your exemplary example. This will set the pace and push your salespeople to their limits.

You must coach them how to sell and how to react to all the objections and rebuttals that will be thrown their way. Be blunt and direct about any shortcomings in their individual selling skills. Communicate and share your dreams, and involve them in setting goals. Guide them in implementing strategies to achieve their own goals.

TIP: A goal is an aspiration combined with specific mileposts. A goal should also have a projected date of accomplishment.

TIP: Break down goals into the specifics—daily activities, numbers, calls, presentations, etc.

Don't let your people set pie in the sky, unachievable goals. Successful goal setting comes from an awareness of real-world realities. Emphasize the work required to achieve what they want, and help them to accomplish these goals.

You have to practice and rehash. Get yourself and your team to analyse each area of the sales process and work on weaknesses.

Practice makes perfect. Rehash the sales process again and again and again. Problem solve any weaknesses that arise. Again, you must be blunt and direct, or you can't expect the team to overcome any shortcomings that will undoubtedly arise. That's the difference between those who make it and those who give up.

Build Your Team's Winning Spirit

Anyone involved with sales is bombarded with negativity. How many no's can salespeople or communicators take before losing their positive outlook and faith in themselves? Therefore, you must always build up your team members' spirits. You must get excited with them. When a sale is made, do not nitpick irrelevant errors. Celebrate the sale.

Concentrate on the positive aspects. Remember that every no makes it possible to move on to the **NEXT** yes. And as we discussed in previous chapters, that also means that you are earning "x" number of dollars each time you make a phone call or "x" number of dollars each time you give a presentation, whether the prospect buys or not! When that "x" value goes up a notch, that's something to celebrate.

TIP: Focus on the positive results of activity—not on potential lost earnings.

As your team's leader, you have to analyse the specific areas your people fall short. You have to believe in each individual's potential in order to build on his or her strengths. They will become successful people within your organization if they feel wanted and are recognized for their efforts.

Here's how you can accomplish this:

- Build rapport with them. Spend time working side by side. Take time to chat with them like you would any business associate.

- Listen. Be giving of your time and your attention.

- A smile sent their way, even when you're busy, builds confidence and rapport.

- Remember their names, individual interests, and the circumstances of their lives.

- Let them "fly" on their own at times. If you're not constantly instructing them or showing them how to do things "the correct" way, they'll build their own problem solving abilities.

- Compliment them often on both personal and professional matters. Share stories from your life with them, and take time to listen to theirs.

- Ask questions. Be interested in your people. Share in each others' lives outside of work, too. An occasional gathering, like picnics, barbecues, informal sporting events, etc., will strengthen teamwork and demonstrate how important they are to you.

People care that you care about them. They are less concerned with what you know or what you've accomplished. Their growing abilities and their increasing strengths will be your reward.

Priority Planning Is a Must

You do not have an option here. If you want to be successful, you have to be organized. You have to plan your time by scheduling your priorities. You have got to make sure that you are a priority planner.

It doesn't have to be complex. One of the world's wealthiest men summed up his time management system like this:

1. Make the list

2. Prioritize the list

3. Do the list

You will avoid disorganization and frustration if you follow a simple process every night before you go to bed. No matter how late it is, take a few moments to make a realistic list of what you want to accomplish the next day. Prioritize this list in the order it should be done. If the items are out of order, simply number them in the side margin. Also write in a reasonable amount of time you'll allot for each listed item.

You will sleep well knowing your next day will be well-ordered. You can also be confident that what needs doing will be done.

Your aim is to stay on track. You must accomplish the things you've determined are important and not be constantly put off balance by "urgent" events or tasks thrown your way.

You will find the strength and clearheadedness to say no to circumstances that pop up and threaten to sidetrack you from your plan. Important matters in your life—family time, business growth planning, phone calls, recruiting, research, presentations, and sales—will be accomplished rather than put on the back burner. This will ease your stress level and clarify your focus.

Procrastination Steals Dreams

Do it now, unless you want to suffer the fate of those who are never able to accomplish what they dream in life. Each time you check an item off your prioritized list or move on to the next activity, you're separating yourself from the masses and moving closer to your goals.

Become a Master Dream Builder

Help the members of your team identify their dreams and teach them how to internalize them. Show them how to take the dreams into their hearts and treat them as if they were already reality.

TIP: Become a master dream builder for yourself and your team.

Share the excitement of their individual dreams, and do not judge them. Their dreams will fire them up, so don't try to change them or tell them they're pursuing the wrong ones. Aspirations you plant will not generate the same passion, fire, and drive that their own dreams will.

Because you won't have an established rapport with your new hires, you'll have to cultivate their aspirations. Teach them a passion for life and what it has to offer. Over time, you'll discover clues about what motivates them. Is it material objects such as jewellery, cars, and fancy homes? Is it fun or recreation? Are they driven to achieve financial stability for themselves and their families?

As you learn more about your new hires, you'll be able to steer their desires into concrete steps of achievement.

TIP: Our dreams for the future determine our actions today.

Dreams or aspirations have to be seen with clarity. They can't be vague notions or generalized ideas of a type of thing you want. To develop a clearly defined dream, you must follow these three steps:

1. Decide.

Destiny is not a matter of chance; it is a matter of choice. Determine what is important to you, and make a decision on your future.

2. Envision.

Develop a clear picture in your mind by first writing a detailed description of your dream.

3. Imagine.

Create a burning desire for attaining what you envisioned. Close your eyes and picture yourself having achieved your dream. Imagine how it will feel. See, touch, and smell your achievements. Logic opens the mind. Feelings open the heart.

Set Your Goals

TIP: A goal is a dream with a deadline.

Share your dreams with the people who have an interest in helping you achieve them. When you can believe it, you can achieve it. Dream, and anything your mind can conceive, you can achieve.

You don't need a staff of thousands of people and a gigantic organization to make it all happen for you. Don't forget, even if it's a small team, each member has been personally selected and groomed by *you*. This alone will give you a step-up towards communicating and achieving your goals.

TIP: A great leader first follows.

A great leader recognizes other leaders and makes room for them.

The communication of your goals and the ability to achieve them will be passed on through the years because you've set up a system for creating leaders in your image. And they, in turn, will duplicate themselves in other future leaders.

Promote the system and your leaders. As a result, your people will recognize your leadership and know they have a strong, solid support network.

Think of each other, talk with each other, and check with your leaders. Be positive about where you are going. Be sensitive to what others are doing, and be a communicator. Find the balance between helping people and not doing for people what they can do for themselves.

TIP: To gain success in life, change the program until you find one that suits what you want.

It's like watching TV. You turn it on because you want to watch, say, *Charlie's Angels*. But the news is on instead. You simply change the program.

There are challenges in small business just as in the corporate world. It is important that you become a student and aficionado of your particular business. Information is power.

Make sure you have as much data, understanding, and knowledge about your business as possible so that your people do not have to take risks. You already know how to make that happen. Use the right methods and the right system.

TIP: You have to associate with people who support your quest towards achievement.

Too often, friends and family members ridicule dreams and aspirations and what people are doing to achieve them. The very people that a person should be able to turn to for moral support and encouragement are often the ones who do their utmost to discourage and derail you.

To counteract this, associate yourself with good, positive management. These are the people who understand your dreams best, because you have handpicked and trained them to help you achieve them.

Loyalty: A Forgotten Quality

In life, there is too little appreciation for one another. It doesn't take very much effort to thank people for what they have done for you, especially if those people have had any sort of major impact on your life.

Loyalty is very much a forgotten quality amongst unthankful people with no natural appreciation for what life gives them. I have devoted my life to self-improvement, and I will not let attributes like loyalty and appreciation die without trying to instill its virtues into others.

While there are many persons to thank for our lot in life, sometimes there are a few that stand out. These are the people that have had a dramatic effect in influencing both your track and success.

It is for that reason I would like to recognize the persons I believe were directly responsible for pointing me in the right direction on my journey to success.

Mrs. Shonnahan was my second grade teacher. She was hard as nails and put the fear of God into me if I didn't do my homework. I give her thanks for instilling in me the idea that when I do something, I should do it well or not at all.

Mr. Stag was my fourth grade schoolteacher who showed me the importance of using discipline as an improvement tool. Doing the hard yards and using any means available to me to improve is the answer if I want to gain the rewards.

Mr. Tony Green was my first and most influential business mentor. He gave me the philosophy for success. I mention Tony throughout the book and how he influenced my life.

The next person is W. Clement Stone, author of the book *The Success System That Never Fails*. He has influenced my life by providing me with the ingredients for success.

Last but not least was Siegfried Konig, a dynamic individual who taught me how to think big with a lucid mind.

These individuals will remain in my mind and heart, and I will always be grateful for the advice and opportunities they gave me.

Make this and all the other lessons in this book your tools for a better life and business. Thanks for having the common sense to make the decision to invest in your future. All the best for your future life.

DAN CAVALLI
The $140 million man

APPENDIX

The Destroyers of Success

THE PAST PROVIDES VALUABLE LESSONS

H as this ever happened to you? You'll be in the middle of something, and suddenly you feel you've been there before. This has happened to me many times.

I remember buying my first block of land. I had just turned nineteen, and I was driving like a maniac along a road in Brisbane feeling like the king of the road. Then my cap blew out of the car window. It was a favourite of mine, so I screeched the tires to stop and went to pick it up.

Barefoot in my purple pants, I headed towards my cap. But I noticed it had landed in a vacant block of land that was for sale. I looked at this in amazement, and I said to myself, "Was this the Cavalli curse, or could it be a friendly omen?"

I walked over the block and a sudden sense of belonging overwhelmed me. The grass under my feet felt like carpet pile. While I didn't know why I wanted this block, I went about trying to purchase it.

The Beginning

This was the beginning of a number of fruitful experiences that taught me valuable business lessons. Have you ever noticed a vacant block of land along the road as you're driving to work, then without warning, one day something is showing itself out of the ground.

This is how it was for me. I had that block for a year, and then I sold it. The new owners tried to get a house built on it as soon as they could. Nothing happened for ages.

Changes

Then I noticed changes after a while. First there were foundations, and then some days later, it was the start of a house as if by magic. In reality, a house doesn't appear overnight, but it does happen by a process over time. This particular lesson destroyed the instant gratification desires that I had developed in my life. My "I want it now–I can't wait for it" type attitude was gone.

It happens this way. The architect goes to work, draws a plan, seeks permission from councils, and obtains permits before a spade is put into the ground. When it is approved, building can commence.

Made to Last

A solid foundation will ensure your building will last a very long time. Depending on the type and size of the construction, the foundations take time to form.

After the foundations are set, the building can commence. The next step is putting in the steelwork and the subflooring. Then you can erect a shell on the outside of the building. Soon you see it coming out of the ground. Then all of a sudden, a building appears.

How long does it take to complete? Depending on the size of the project, it can take less than two years, and sometimes it only takes one year or even six months. The majority of the work, however, is in the foundation.

Effort and Activity Guarantees You Success

With building, you've already encountered problems and obstacles before you start. But your effort and activity guarantees you success just as in the example of the building above.

This is the easiest way to make a strategy work. Success is based on the time it takes to develop rather than the time it has in experiencing success. In the early days of your business, you'll see no change. There will be no evidence of your dream becoming reality.

Yet it has cost a lot of time, money, and effort to get so far. Often you say to yourself, is this worth it? I can't seem to make it work.

TIP: Hang in there, and it will come together.

It Takes Time

There is a saying in business. It takes three years to establish a business and three days to tear it down. That's why we have these sad statistics that up to 80 percent of businesses fail in the first five years. They have given up because in those first years, they've had too little capital and skill to sustain themselves.

TIP: All the preparation and hard work must be done first with very little evidence of success.

Only then will you see the fruits of your labour.

Most people give in before they see the evidence of their success because they can't see the bigger picture. There are a number of qualities achievers possess. Perhaps the most prominent is desire.

Another necessary ingredient for success is persistence. This coupled with desire will create the best effect. As you work toward your dreams, you may become tired and grow weary. We grow weary or stronger depending on where we are in life.

SUCCESS IS A HABIT

Success is closely tied to the habits you develop. It is unbelievable that the majority of people spend their lives wanting to be successful and yet never attain it. Why?

TIP: I blame parents for many of the traits we see in our youth today.

Many parents are hypocrites as they say they love their children by being kind to them. It takes more effort than that, as you will see.

Every day I experience the difference between a good mother or father and a good parent. Sometimes it's being the good mum or dad that is the greatest injustice to a child. The difference between the two is significant.

Weak Parents

A good mum or dad will protect the child from harm. It's the kiss and cuddle cliché without the instruction that should accompany it. The good parent part of rearing a family is the teaching and instruction, including the pain and reward method.

Being a good parent teaches children how to survive and be successful in life.

The saddest part is that most people with average ability can succeed to a certain degree if they duplicate some of the strategies they have read about here. But they just don't do it.

TIP: If your parents weren't tough enough on you as a child to teach you these lessons, it is up to you to make the lessons work for yourself.

It doesn't matter where people are right now or where they have been. They can succeed and build a large profitable business if they only develop the right kind of habits. This is far easier said than done, but I'll show you how.

Tradition

What is the traditional thinking about success? Take note. These words are equal to knowing the gold lotto numbers because it ties together the attributes desire and persistence in its definition.

TIP: My definition of success is being able to think, act, and correct your course while maintaining control of the activity required to achieve your goal.

Success was traditionally synonymous with wealth. But there are a lot of unhappy millionaires who would say they are not successful.

There are many people around with no money who are not happy or successful. Not everyone wants a business that earns them thousands of dollars a week or the hard work that goes with that. Money is a sign of how well our goals are turning to reality.

If you were to interview some of the wealthiest people in the world, they would probably tell you that making a lot of money was not their primary objective when they set out on their journeys to success.

Make no mistake about it. This single factor of not having money as your motivator alone has the power to move you to great heights. It will give you the reason to get out of bed each day and give you enjoyable long hours of energy.

Desire

I remember as a boy I had a fetish for catching possums. I'd spend hours setting the trap at night, and in the morning, I'd race out to see what I had caught. When the trap was empty, I'd jump up and down, cry, scream, and carry on like a spoiled child. Then I'd take it out on whoever I saw that day. I wanted instant gratification.

The desire to catch a possum was great. In some ways, I was starting to learn. Even though I wanted results there and then, I developed persistence.

TIP: I started to try some other types of traps. It may have been a snare made of copper wire or a trick stick that would fall once the possum was in the cage. Whatever I tried, it didn't seem to work.

I kept this up week after week. Any normal kid would have given up after a week or so, but not me. I would get a renewed strength by the anticipation of the next day's excitement.

The more I tried, the more I failed. Then one day, I discovered another of life's lessons. I sat down and actually thought about what I was doing.

Thinking Time

In business, it's the same. You need to stop and spend time thinking about your business. If you have your eyes too closely focused on the present, the future tends to blur. To continue doing something the same way and expect a different result is a loose definition of madness.

Being short-sighted means you are more interested in the immediate rather than the long-term effects of what you are doing. When your plan is well-defined, pursued dreams and goals direct your life towards positive achievement.

Your vision, dreams, and goals will be lost unless you act. Have you put together an action plan to help you reach some of your primary dreams and goals? If not, ask yourself why not? Do one as soon as possible.

Once you have done these things, you must make sure that your dream doesn't get away. Let's go back to the possum story through examination and reexamination of how the possum got away. I discovered a major problem. I actually caught a possum many times in the trap, but I couldn't keep it caught.

After many days of frustration, I saw the problem and solution. I was just about to wake from my sleep one morning when it hit me like a ton of bricks.

TIP: Ideas come to you in the middle of the night, so keep a notebook beside your bed to record them. Otherwise you'll forget them by morning.

Even though there was no possum in the trap, I knew I had actually caught one from the evident scratch marks on the ground. Analysing the problem and not the trap was the answer. I found that it was in the last stage of building the trap that I was ineffective.

The bottom of the trap had no protection to stop the possum from getting out once it was caught. So I put a piece of canvass across the bottom and fixed buttons all around the edges of the trap. Then I buttoned up the escape area with canvas to prevent the possum from getting out.

This is where the expression "the button up" came from. (The button up is an expression taught in my sales training courses to confirm a sale.) From then on, I caught and kept as many possums as I wished. I had learned my lesson well. This was also a great lesson in business for me years later.

Easy

It is not easy because the all-important qualities for success are desire and persistence. It requires some serious effort to make a successful business. Most people, though, are beaten before they even start. For them, it's easier not to try at all.

Let me give you an example of what I mean. If you were asked to stand a raw egg on its end without being supported, would it be achievable? Try it if you're not sure. Get a raw egg and stand it on its end.

Now listen to your thoughts after you've tried it for a while. Are you saying to yourself, "It's way too hard" or "It's impossible?" Most people would say that after trying only once rather than a few times.

However, it is easy. Simply hit the egg on its end and crush the shell!

Hunting Ducks

Let me tell you another lesson I learned in my life. I was about seventeen years of age when I decided to go hunting for wild duck on the Andromacia River in North Queensland. The river was well-known for the crocodiles and ducks that frequented there.

I put my rifle inside the case and slipped it under my right leg beside the engine of my Triumph 650cc tiger 110 (ex-cop bike) and headed to the Andromacia River. I parked the bike about 100 metres from the northern bank and prepared for the hunt.

Now just picture this. Here I was in the paddock with frost beneath my flying boots on this cold winter day. I was dressed in a pair of old railway felt pants that covered me all the way from my waist to the wet grass. Over my chest I had a woolen jumper and a motorbike jacket as well.

Teaching

My parents were the best mum and dad. They fussed over me, and on cold days, they said I had to rug up and keep warm. But they were not the best parents on this occasion. Never once did they teach me about going hunting in cold weather near water, which was a common practice in that area. So let's find out how this affected me on this occasion.

Young and impetuous as I was, I crawled through the grass on my elbows and knees to reach the water's edge. I peered through the bushes on the weathered bank and saw my first ducks.

Without hesitation, I shot. It rang out across the water and hit its mark. The duck managed to swim into the reeds to hide. I couldn't leave a wounded bird to die, so I took off my boots and jumped in to retrieve it.

Dangers

I got over to the duck and grabbed it. I turned and went back towards the bank. What I hadn't been told was that the clothes I was wearing were dangerous.

They began to soak up the water and became heavier and heavier. Panic set in and breaststroke turned into a frantic dog paddle. I began to sink, and no matter how hard I tried to keep my head above the water, I couldn't. So I sank.

Down I went until I couldn't see the surface light, and although it was only a few metres deep, it seemed ages until I hit the bottom. All I could think of as my mind went into slow motion was that the Cavalli curse finally got me.

I moved along the river floor towards the bank on my hands and knees and hoped to make it. Finally arriving, I dragged myself up the side of the bank. Totally exhausted, I lay freezing and thinking how lucky I was to be alive. I celebrated that night with roast duck and veggies, and I pondered about the Cavalli curse.

Now it's time to start putting this information into practice. Analyse what lessons can be learned from the duck story. These lessons can help you also.

TIP: Most people are beaten before they even start.

It is not easy, because the all-important quality for success is persistence. It's called survival.

It's something that must be taught. Most parents don't spend enough time with their kids. Some don't believe in homework for kids. I do. Who knows what is right with the changing view points of authorities these days? But it's setting aside the time to spend with them that's important.

Play Time

Play time is important, but so is time where parents teach their kids to learn, to like study, to like education, and to learn the reward and pain principles. And kids can learn these things from as young as three years of age. That's what is important.

The moral of this story is that to be able to stand on your own two feet, you have to hit your head sometimes in order to learn from your experience. Simple! Put that "learned experience" into action.

TIP: You can put some blame on your patents for not teaching you how to do well. But as an adult, the responsibility to learn is yours.

Childhood Lessons That Sabotage Success

Let's talk about another destroyer of success. It's a concept taught to us as children.

From an early age, we're told that if we wish to be liked and have friends, we must share our toys. We're instructed to not be selfish. So when other kids came to your home, it was assumed they had a right to our toys, puzzles, games, and other personal possessions. This was a concept enforced by our parents. We're taught to conform in the interest of maintaining harmony.

But what is the message? It's not that there's value in sharing or learning how to get along with others who matter to us. Unfortunately, the real message passed on is far less altruistic. It's that we must be obedient to be socially accepted. We're taught that if we please others, we will be liked in return.

In order to please our parents, we had to be obedient. To please our teachers, family members, and other adults, we had to be well-behaved. The underlying message was always the same. We're supposed to like others, regardless of their worth, and we must strive to be liked in return.

I'm not making a case against sharing or learning how to behave in the social world. My point is that, from a young age, we're brainwashed with the idea that we have to be liked to fit in. We should conform and never make waves. We should seek precious little else in life than approval.

This is hardly a formula for success. I hope that by making yourself aware of this, it will cause you to challenge yourself when you find you're focusing too much on attaining the approval of others. I also hope it will cause you to look at how we raise our children. Remember, if we make the wrong decision about this, our children will likely pay the price when they're adults.

Preparing Kids for Their Future

The interesting thing about the river episode is that I still had the duck in my hand and never again spoke of the Cavalli curse. I had discovered how to develop persistence to benefit my life. I now called it the Cavalli's Cure.

Many people have no clue whether they are better off on wages or being self-employed. Are you better off being on wages or self-employed? It will depend on your situation.

I'm not talking about the position you are in financially. Rather, I'm dealing with how you are prone to mind conditioning. This is another parent's obligation to teach their children that has been neglected.

Parents are lazy when it comes to really helping and preparing their kids for their future life. Sure, when someone picks on their little girl or boy at school or treats them unfairly, parents will rush to their side to support them in their trials and tribulations. But what does that alone teach your child?

Difficulty

What rubbish! It's then that kids need the opposite reaction from their parents. They need someone to teach them how to overcome their adversity.

TIP: Teach them to stand on their own two feet. Teach them channels by which they can find the necessary assistance.

But that's too hard for ignorant parents! It's easier to show kids how, in some cases, they embarrass themselves with arguments and yelling at people for upsetting their precious little child.

More Destroyers of Success

To uncover an enemy's intentions is to disarm them. Many believe that the wealthy are invulnerable to attack from competitors, from those who are envious, or from those wishing to profit from their misfortune. Nothing can be further from the truth.

For a person to succeed today they must be constantly vigilant and streetwise, because you can bet their enemies will be. So how do we identify these threats and create systems that will protect us against them? We can't possibly tackle that issue until we know who or what to protect our assets from.

First of all, throw away the stereotypes. It's no longer obvious, blatant, sleazy con men you have to watch out for. Modern attackers are much more insidious, because they hide behind national or international organizations operating under various trade names.

It may be an unscrupulous government official, or worse, it could be another company's employee.

The way these people treat you can have disastrous effects on your business finances. They may even maneuver you into bankruptcy. They are the "sharks" of the business world.

Sharks Hunger for Your Assets

It's impossible to avoid this type of carnivore if you participate in the financial world. Sharks are after one thing and one thing only. They're after your assets. Don't ever lose sight of that.

True, their actions may have been sparked by something you said or perhaps an old grudge. Maybe you won something that they coveted, or perhaps they just don't like the way you look! It doesn't matter why. It all boils down to the same thing—they want to make you suffer, they want to control you, and they want to make you pay. They'll attempt to accomplish this by attacking your financial assets.

And their weapon of choice is usually the legal system.

It could be something as minor and seemingly insignificant as outstanding parking fines. In many municipalities, one can be jailed for such infractions, and you'll be housed right alongside hardened criminals. Perhaps they'll attack through a country's tax authority or securities/investment exchange commissions.

And don't forget that these allegations don't need to be true. The authorities will still have to investigate the complaint. Even if it never goes beyond that point, it's still going to prove distracting, time-consuming, embarrassing, and often costly.

We see it every day on television—someone accuses another, and the media has a field day with the story. When people make false claims, it can still result in financial hardship and destroy hard-earned reputations. The only way to handle such attacks is by returning fire with a vengeance. Even if they're much weaker than you, if they combine with their allies, they can wreak havoc. So your survival depends on not holding back.

TIP: When others attack you, retaliate through the legal system. Be noisy about it, and involve the media until they leave you alone.

Treachery Hides behind Masks

If you have a problem with staff or personal relationships but can't put your finger on what is exactly the problem, here is a simple solution to point you in the right direction. Look for the nicest person that is close to you and investigate his or her behaviour. The answer is there!

I have worked with many people, but none started out nicer than the one I'll call Tom. Tom was always courteous and helpful. He started work before everyone else and left long after the others had gone. We all knew that when there was a task that absolutely had to get done, Tom was the man to see it through.

In fact, quite often when I'd leave the office, he would ask how long I'd be gone so he could have a particular job completed by my return. Tom was in my employ for two years, and we trusted him implicitly.

During that same two-year period, some of the staff reported their wallets or purses missing, and occasionally fifty dollars from petty cash would somehow end up unaccounted for. These incidents were investigated, but to no avail, and none of the missing money was ever found.

One day my wife commented that, according to the balances, I was spending a lot of our personal cash at work, sometimes as much as $500 a week. This was an unusually large amount for us to go through weekly, yet somehow I couldn't place what I had spent it on.

I began to take note of exactly how much I spent, and I also did an audit on my wallet every hour on the hour for three days. As expected, on day one $200 was missing, on day two it was $80, and day three $180.

Suspicion Followed by Mistrust

A couple of days later, as I was leaving for a meeting, Tom stopped me to ask how long I would be out of the office. I told him I planned to be gone about an hour. But I hadn't gone more than about 50 metres when I realized I'd left my cell phone on my desk. I had to go back to get it.

Now I rarely close my office door unless I'm in a meeting, so it struck me as odd when I found it shut. I opened the door, and Tom was in there.

"I thought I'd clean your desk for you," Tom told me in answer to my puzzled look.

After he left, I found myself wondering why he found it necessary to shut my door if he was merely cleaning my desk. I checked my wallet, and there was fifty dollars missing. I felt a knot in my stomach. It just couldn't be Tom.

This thought plagued me for the next few days, and the only way to clear my head of doubt was to find out for sure. I didn't confront Tom directly in case I was wrong. He was such a good employee, and we all liked him. I hired a surveillance team who installed hidden cameras into the ceiling of my office late at night when our offices were otherwise empty. The next day, my heart was racing in anticipation of what I would find on the tapes.

A Shark Attacking Its Prey

I was determined to find the culprit but hoped in my heart it wasn't Tom. I left my wallet in the usual place (in my briefcase on the floor) after putting in ten $100 notes. I marked each with a cross on the bottom left-hand corner. I told Tom I was going out, and I'd be back in an hour.

Upon my return, with my mind racing and heart pounding, I gathered up our operations manager to accompany me to my office. Together we replayed the video, and sure enough, there he was. Tom had my briefcase open and was pocketing my money.

I felt sick to my stomach as I watched the smooth, swift manner in which he committed the crime. A vision came to mind of a shark attacking its prey before fading off into the deep.

Do yourself a favour and reread this section. Give someone the benefit of the doubt if they deserve it. But never forget to beware of "the nice guy." If they are overly friendly, it's a sign that you should watch your back.

When I confronted Tom about the theft, he was so nice about how the situation was handled. I even had second thoughts about reporting the incident. I recovered from this incident, but it was nothing short of heartbreaking. And it was a lesson well learned.

Criminologists tell us that most violent crimes, like rape, murder, or molestation, are perpetrated by people who are close to the victims and occupy a position of trust. In other words, the perpetrator is likely someone the victim found nice and trustworthy.

There's a valuable lesson in this. We have to see through the lies and scams we come across every day. You have to become an expert at recognizing the con men and build up a fortress against their devious ways.

Otherwise, the fruits of all our hard work and the financial well-being of those who depend on us may be lost forever.

ABOUT THE AUTHOR

Daniel Cavalli has no formal university education, but he does have an impressive background in business management. He has experience in sales training methodology both academically and through practical experience.

Daniel's enthusiasm, passion for business, and personal integrity have enabled him to attract quality people in his own business and have ensured a loyal, professional management team. His performance in training and coaching salespeople and sales teams has earned him numerous awards.

The marketing strategy and training programs Daniel has developed for companies have enabled his sales trainers to turn enthusiastic and dedicated beginners into successful sales representatives in just a few months.

DAN CAVALLI ASKS: WHAT QUALIFIES ME AS THE EXPERT, AND WHY SHOULD YOU LISTEN TO WHAT I HAVE TO SAY?

What makes me different from most other business marketers? There are hundreds of people out there claiming to know all the answers. There are few who can back up their claims. This is my story:

I was in the same boat as you are now. I tried every product and idea I could get my hands on, but I couldn't make it. Everything I tried was either too hard to follow or too expensive.

The worst part was that I was gullible, because I believed everything I read about getting ahead. I have spent thousands of dollars and hundreds of hours staring blankly at the computer wondering how long before my business took off. As the days went on, I became even more frustrated. I was losing heart.

As it turned out, this was the situation I found myself in. I was missing the most important skill any business (especially online) must develop, which is how to attract, sell to, and keep prospects.

Who did I want to learn from? I wanted to learn from someone who had already done what I wanted to do. I wanted someone who started from nothing and went on to become extremely successful in his particular field. I wanted someone who could teach me how to achieve his results, and I wanted someone who could condense everything he knew into easy to follow steps. These are the masters of marketing. They are the ones to notice, but they are hard to identify.

When I overcame these problems, my whole world instantly changed for the better. My desire to succeed in my own automatic moneymaking business grew, and before long, I was on my way. Over the next few years, I drafted all of these skills into easy-to-understand systems. Eventually I found the courage to stop working for others. I decided to start my own business to see what I could do with my experience and knowledge. I put my system and knowledge to the test.

The rest is history. I started a business from scratch, and within eighteen months, I had built an organization with a turnover of $140 million. A colleague said to me one day, "Anyone with a little luck and know-how can do that if everything falls into their lap."

I started wondering whether what I had done was a fluke. Was success really achieved by applying my principles and techniques? So I sold that business and started another one. This second business also turned over in excess of $10 million in a short time.

I know now that it isn't a fluke but rather the techniques and strategies that are implemented. This is my experience and qualifications as the expert. I learned my lessons well and can tell you what they are. I now have a story to tell you.

PERSONAL PROFILE

PROFILE: DANIEL CAVALLI

EDUCATION: Year 8

FIRST YEAR IN BUSINESS: 1995

TYPE OF BUSINESS: Telecommunications

TARGET MARKET: Small to Medium Businesses

NUMBER OF EMPLOYEES: Fifteen

BEST MONTH (GROSS REVENUE): $18 Million

HOURS WORKED PER WEEK DURING START-UP PHASE: Sixty hours

HOURS WORKED PER WEEK NOW: Fifteen to twenty hours, by choice

FAVOURITE BUSINESS BOOKS:

The Success System That Never Fails - by W. Clement Stone
Mean Business - by Al Dunlap
The Prince – by Niccolo Machiavelli - Penguin Classics edition
The New Machiavelli – by Alistair McAlpine
The 48 Laws of Power - by Robert Greene

RELAXATION ACTIVITIES: Writing – Reading – Motorcycle Riding - Travel

PHYSICAL ACTIVITIES: Running – Cycling - Gym

FAVOURITE PART OF THE JOB: Documentation of policies and systems

LEAST FAVOURITE PART OF THE JOB: Physically uploading information onto the Internet

COMPANIES ADMIRED: Telcoblue

FAVOURITE QUOTES:

> "Whatever one man can do, another can do" – Anthony Hopkins from *The Edge*

> "If there is nothing to lose by trying and a great deal to gain if successful, by all means try" – W. Clement Stone (CICA)

PEOPLE ADMIRED: Those who can lose weight. Those who can stay successful in business. Those who believe in and promote accountability.

WHO AGITATES ME: Parents who don't teach their children to be accountable. People who accept injustice. People who can be better but don't try hard enough.

HEROES: Anyone who beats the odds

ACCOMPLISHMENTS: Going from zero to multimillions in my first business then repeating that again in my second and third businesses

----

Books/Reports Authored:

The 26 Greatest Mistakes of All Time in Achieving Success

The 9 Imperative Questions To Ask If You Are Starting a Business

Exploding Your Business in Less Than Three Months

The Key to Abundance

What It Takes To Build A Million Dollar Business

The Dynamic Business Management to Personal Development

The Dynamic Business Management to Sales Training

The Telcoblue eCourse sales training modules

Getting Started Tips: Don't spend a cent until you educate yourself in what, where, and how you are going to conduct every aspect of your business.

View on technology: I use it as soon as it is proven to work.

Do you use auto responders? Yes

How do you market on the Internet? Through others, never myself

Marketing Techniques: Telephone, newspapers, calls centres, direct mail, Internet, and websites

----

Your View on Partnerships: It depends. If it's a real life partnership, stay away from it. If it's a JV on the Internet, go for it. Stay away from personal business relationships.

Your View on Hiring Family Members: It depends. If they can do as they're told without fuss, they're hired! If they can't, no!

WHEN LEGAL ISSUES ARISE, WHAT'S YOUR USUAL RESPONSE? Get a legal opinion, and if I have more than a 50 percent chance of winning, I go for it. If less than 50 percent, I move on to the NEXT opportunity.

ADVANTAGES OF EARNING A LOT OF MONEY: Doing what you want when you want

DISADVANTAGES: Let's put it in perspective. There are no legitimate disadvantages.

BEST GENERAL TAX ADVICE: Get yourself a good conservative accountant

BEST GENERAL INVESTMENT ADVICE: Stay away from all stock exchanges, shares, and investment planners. Invest in bricks and mortar and in yourself.

YOU'RE IN BUSINESS ALREADY, AND YOU'VE JUST RECEIVED A WINDFALL OF $100,000. WHAT WOULD YOU DO WITH IT? Use it to assist me in buying another house.

WHAT MOTIVATES YOU TO CONTINUE BUILDING YOUR BUSINESS? Lifestyle

----

WHAT'S THE BEST THING ABOUT BEING SELF-EMPLOYED? Doing what you want when you want

THE MOST UNDERRATED ACTIVITY IN BUSINESS IS . . . Building an effective marketing and lead generation plan

THE MOST OVERRATED ACTIVITY IN BUSINESS IS . . . Implementing a business plan

WHAT WAS THE BIGGEST OBSTACLE YOU HAD TO FACE WHEN YOU WERE LAUNCHING YOUR OWN BUSINESS? Having enough cash flow

WHAT'S YOUR BIGGEST OBSTACLE NOW? Having enough cash flow

IF YOU HAD TO START YOUR BUSINESS ALL OVER AGAIN, WHAT WOULD YOU DO DIFFERENTLY? Nothing

WHAT CAUSED YOUR WORST BUSINESS DECISION? Being too emotional about it and not making the decision from a commercial point of view

WHAT WAS YOUR BEST BUSINESS DECISION? When I decided to learn about the selling game and personal development

----

WHAT DO YOU CONSIDER TO BE THE MAIN KEYS TO YOUR SUCCESS? The ability to make a decision about a good deal quickly

WHAT'S YOUR SUCCESS PHILOSOPHY? The money in the bank measures success

HOW HAS SUCCESS IN BUSINESS CHANGED YOU? I find I am becoming more of an expert without the stress

WHAT LEGACY DO YOU HOPE TO LEAVE? The books I have written

BONUS LINKS

 "140 Million Insider Secrets" a $140 million business enterprise's worst nightmare, exposed as a special condensed eBook. Immediate download:

> http://www.commandobusiness.com/pdf/
> zero_to_140_million_in_18_months.pdf

"Free" 40 Minute interview with Shawn Nelson and Dan Cavalli… the $140 million dollar man discussing life and/or business. Immediate download:

> http://www.goldstarmember.com/mp3/Shawn_Nelson.mp3

"No Holds Barred" interview with #1 best-selling author Mike Litman. Immediate download:

> http://www.goldstarmember.com/mp3/ML_Dan_Cavalli_GU_October.mp3